The Private World of GEORGETTE HEYER

Jane Aiken Hodge has written twenty-one historical novels, eight contemporary detective stories, a life of Jane Austen and a study of the lives of Regency women. Born in America, she grew up in England but also worked for the British Government in Washington D.C. and *Time Magazine* in New York. Married twice, she has two daughters and two granddaughters and now lives in Lewes, Sussex.

Praise for *The Private World of Georgette Heyer*

'One of the most beautiful books I know. Time and time again, on reading this book, I found myself breaking off to lift another dog-eared Heyer from the shelf and lose myself in the increased pleasure of a re-reading . . . A successful biography'
Washington Post Book World

'A fascinating biography of Georgette Heyer, one that deserves reading just as much as Heyer's novels'
Courier Mail

Also available by Jane Aiken Hodge

Fiction
Maulever Hall
The Adventurers
Watch the Wall, My Darling
Here Comes a Candle
The Winding Stair
Greek Wedding
Marry in Haste
Savannah Purchase
Strangers in Company
Shadow of a Lady
One Way to Venice
Rebel Heiress
Runaway Bride
Judas Flowering
Red Sky at Night
Last Act
Wide is the Water
The Lost Garden
Secret Island
Polonaise
First Night
Leading Lady
Bride of Dreams
Unsafe Hands
Susan in America
Caterina
A Death in Two Parts
Deathline

Non-fiction
Only a Novel: The Double Life of Jane Austen
Passion and Principle: The Loves and Lives of Regency Women

The Private World of GEORGETTE HEYER

JANE AIKEN HODGE

arrow books

This edition published in the United Kingdom by Arrow Books in 2006

5 7 9 10 8 6 4

First published in the United Kingdom in 1984 by The Bodley Head Ltd
First published in paperback in 1985 by Pan Books Ltd

Arrow Books
The Random House Group Limited
20 Vauxhall Bridge Road, London, SW1V 2SA

www.randomhouse.co.uk

Addresses for companies within The Random House Group Limited can be found
at: www.randomhouse.co.uk/offices.htm

The Radnom House Group Limited Reg. No. 954009

A CIP catalogue record for this book
is available from the British Library

ISBN 9780099493495

The Random House Group Limited makes every effort to ensure that the papers
used in its books are made from trees that have been legally sourced from
well-managed and credibly certified forests. Our paper procurement policy can be
found at: www.randomhouse.co.uk/paper.htm

Typeset by SX Composing DTP, Rayleigh, Essex
Printed and bound in Great Britain by
Bookmarque Ltd, Croydon, Surrey

To Georgette Heyer
alias Mrs Ronald Rougier

Acknowledgements

I am deeply grateful to Richard and Susie Rougier, who made this book possible, and to Frank Heyer. I am also indebted to the following friends, relatives and associates of Georgette Heyer who made me free of their memories and lent me their letters from her: Mrs Isabella Banton, Mrs Enid Chasemore, Mrs Jane Chester, Mr Hale Crosse, Mrs E. G. Delaforce, Mr and Mrs A. S. Frere, Mr Elliot Graham, Canon and Mrs Heyman, Mrs Ruby Hill, Mrs Deborah Owen, Mr and Mrs Max Reinhardt, Mr and Mrs Donald Sinden, Mr John Smith, Mr and Mrs Dmitri Tornow, Colonel and Mrs John Weaver, Miss Joyce Weiner, Mrs Valerie Worth.

I also wish to thank for their help: Mrs Paddy Aiken, Mrs Claire Barwell, Mrs Thelma Baynon, Headmistress of The Study, Mr A. E. Bradley, Principal of Westminster College, Mrs A. S. Byatt, Miss Grace Cranston, Archivist of Heinemann, Dr J. A. Edwards, Archivist of the University of Reading Library, Mr Simon Lawrence, Mr Eric Major of Hodder & Stoughton, Mr Douglas Matthews, Librarian of the London Library, Mrs Maureen May, Mr Frank Miles, Archivist of King's College School, Mrs Anne Oliver, Miss Julia Trevelyan Oman, Mrs A. A. Piper, Headmistress of Wimbledon High School, Mrs Pauline Prest of the Wimbledon Literary and Scientific Society, Miss Joy Preston, Miss Josephine Pullein-Thompson, Mr T. J. Rix of Longman, Mrs Jane Fane de Salis, Mr P. J. Shaw, Miss Peggy Sutherland, the Imperial War Museum and the National Army Museum.

I am grateful to Joanna Cannan's family for permission to quote from *No Walls of Jasper*, and to The Bodley Head and William Heinemann for permission to quote from Georgette Heyer's novels, and above all to Jill Black of Bodley Head for friendly and constructive editing, and for the pictures. I am also most grateful to Georgette Heyer's devoted readers for their appreciative letters about the hardback of this book, and their constructive comments, which have been incorporated into the text.

Foreword

Georgette Heyer was an intensely private person. A best-seller all her life without the aid of publicity, she made no appearances, never gave an interview, and only answered fan letters herself if they made an interesting historical point. Having scored an instant success with *The Black Moth* at the age of nineteen under her own name, Georgette Heyer, she experimented with a pseudonym, Stella Martin, for her third book, published by Mills & Boon, then achieved a permanent alias when she married Ronald Rougier at twenty-three. From then on, Georgette Heyer wrote the best-sellers, while Mrs Ronald Rougier led the deeply private life. She never talked about her background and early years, giving only the barest facts of her life in eighteen lines of *Who's Who*. After her death, A. S. Byatt, the critic and novelist, wrote an invaluable long memorial piece for the *Sunday Times*, based on interviews with her husband, her friend Carola Oman and her two good publisher friends, A. S. Frere of Heinemann and Max Reinhardt of The Bodley Head. This is the only source for much of the information about her early life, about which she herself never talked. I have been able to supplement it by talking to her surviving family and friends (her husband and Carola Oman are now both dead) and by reference to her letters and to the four early novels she later suppressed.

Her own invariable answer, when asked about her private life, was to refer the questioner back to her books. You will find me, she said, in my work. So should one now, almost ten years after her death, try to look behind the curtain of privacy in which she

Georgette Heyer in 1946. 'It was thought to be a speaking likeness,' she wrote nostalgically in 1964, 'even my life's companion approving of it and setting up a copy on his desk in Chambers.'

shrouded herself? My first instinct, when I started work on this book, was to concentrate entirely on the work, merely giving the barest facts of her life as a foreword. Then I began to talk to the people who knew her, and to read her letters. Everyone who knew her had loved or respected her, and they all seemed glad that a book should be written about her. But her own letters settled the question. She may have been a private person socially, almost a recluse, but on paper she was a compulsive communicator. And she wrote, her son says, just as she talked. Her letters to her publishers are full of sidelights on her own life and pungent comments on the world at large. They confirm, in short, her friends' unanimous description of her as shy on the surface, but a formidable, positive person underneath, with strong views and a great sense of style.

It hardly sounds the description of a purveyor of romantic froth. But in fact, for those with eyes to see, the strong character is there in her books, even in the lightest and most frivolous of them, and an awareness of the kind of person she was adds a new dimension to one's enjoyment of them, or, perhaps, helps to explain just why one does enjoy them. She may have been a compulsive writer, but she was also an immensely skilled and meticulous craftswoman. She did her best to conceal her high standards and stern moral code behind the mask of romantic comedy, and succeeded, so far as her great fan public was concerned. But she had a smaller audience, among dons and journalists, among her husband's legal associates, among intelligent women everywhere, and even among feminists, who enjoyed the romantic syllabub all the more because they were aware of the hard core of realism underneath.

Naturally, it was the ravening fan public that made its voice most clearly heard during her lifetime, and its adulation served both to drive her further into herself and to put off readers who might have enjoyed her as they do Jane Austen or even Ivy Compton-Burnett, a favourite of hers. There is a terrible snobbery in the average intellectual reaction to her work. It is not everyone who has given her name to a type of novel, and it is unfortunate that that name should tend to provoke an uninformed, unjustified sneer. My aim in this book is to try to redress the balance by giving a feeling of her and of her work, as far as possible through her own words in the extensive correspondence which her publishers have kindly made available to me and her letters to friends. Some of her friends, though happy to talk about Georgette Heyer, have felt that she would not have wished her letters shown or quoted, and this is a feeling that must be respected. Her letters to her publishers, on the other hand, are part of the professional world she enjoyed, and unless otherwise indicated all the quotations in this book are from them.

Unfortunately, hardly any letters survive from before the 1940s, when she herself was in her forties and had been a bestseller for years. By this time she was taking a sadly deprecatory line about her own work. Speaking of *Friday's Child* in 1943 she says: 'Spread the glad tidings that it will not disappoint Miss Heyer's many admirers. Judging from the letters I've received from obviously feeble-minded persons who do so wish I could write another *These Old Shades*, it ought to sell like hot cakes. I think myself I ought to be shot for writing such nonsense, but it's unquestionably good escapist literature, and I think I should rather like it if I were sitting in an air-raid shelter, or recovering from flu. Its period detail is good; my husband says it's witty – and without going to these lengths, I will say that it is very good fun.'

The statement sums up the problem she had with her readers. The dons and lawyers mostly kept quiet. The more vociferous of the fans tended to like the wrong books for the wrong reasons. They kept asking for swashbuckling romance when she was writing neat romantic comedy in the vein of Congreve and Sheridan. The reviewers, too, failed to appreciate the style and craftsmanship of her work as it developed into what would be known as 'the Georgette Heyer'. It is no wonder that she turned against publicity of any kind.

As well as the letters, Georgette Heyer left the unfinished typescript of about half of what she had planned as a serious mediaeval book, since published as *My Lord John*; a remarkable

A page from one of Georgette Heyer's Regency notebooks. She knew every detail of the Great North Road, but no heroine of hers ever actually got to Gretna Green.

research library of some thousand volumes (now unfortunately dispersed); and a small but highly significant collection of papers, to which her son has kindly given me access. There was no attic full of carefully hoarded manuscripts and first drafts. A flat-dweller since 1939, she found the proliferating copies of her published books problem enough without indulging in the sentiment of keeping old papers, however fascinating they might have proved to posterity. She saved a few reviews, and one fan letter. It was from a woman who had kept herself and her cell-mates sane through twelve years in a Romanian political prison by telling the story of *Friday's Child* over and over again.

There was an impressive collection of her own research material. About three-quarters of this was the detailed and meticulous work for what was to become *My Lord John*. The rest, even more immediately fascinating, consists of the files devoted to research for her eighteenth-century and Regency novels. There is also a group of short stories that have never been published except in magazine form; two articles published in

Punch and one from the *Sphere*, and five articles that have never been published at all. The stories are typical Heyers, and it is surprising that they have not been published as a companion volume to *Pistols for Two*, but Georgette Heyer never thought much of her short stories, dismissing them as mere pot-boilers. The articles – critical, personal and political – are an interesting experiment that apparently did not come off. We should probably be grateful. If *Punch* had gone on publishing her in 1954 we might have gained an essayist and lost some of her best work.

She might have turned 'respectable'. After its heyday in the nineteenth century, the historical novel had fallen into disrepute in the early years of the twentieth, and this was particularly true when Georgette Heyer started to write. She herself was obviously influenced by popularizers like Baroness Orczy and Jeffery Farnol, but they had helped to give the genre a vulgar name. Her planned book about John, Duke of Bedford, was to be respectable: a very early example of the more serious kind of historical novel that would be developed by people like Zoë Oldenbourg and Mary Renault.

Her books may not have received critical acclaim, but they sold. When she died, at seventy-one, in 1974, she had fifty-one titles in print in hard covers or paperback and had been translated into at least ten languages and pirated in others. She was that rare thing, a steady best-seller. Hyped single titles come and go. Even in the current climate of sex and violence, her books are still solidly on the shelves. In fact, she now has more titles in print than she did when she died, since *My Lord John* has been published and *Simon the Coldheart*, an early historical novel, reprinted. Her name is a household word, used in *The Times* crossword puzzle in the Thirties and in the *New York Times* one in 1982. She is a literary phenomenon that demands investigation.

I have indulged myself, for the purposes of this book, in reading her entire output in chronological order and it has proved a rewarding experience as well as a delightful one. There are, to begin with, four early novels which she later suppressed. *Instead of the Thorn*, *Helen*, *Pastel* and *Barren Corn* were all written in her late teens and early twenties and are about the experiences

Axford and Paragon Buildings, Bath. Heyer heroines were apt to be depressed in gossip-ridden Bath. Kitten, in Friday's Child, *missed her husband, and Lady Serena, in* Bath Tangle, *missed her hunting and her father.*

of young women growing up in the complex social scene of the years after the First World War. Inevitably they and the detective stories she wrote mainly in her thirties throw a certain amount of light on the early years of her own life about which she would never talk. Her surviving brother, Frank Heyer, has confirmed that there is a considerable autobiographical element in the novels, particularly in *Helen*.

What she did not choose to write about is almost as interesting as what she did. Like Jane Austen, she knew her own limitations to a nicety. She spent the early years of her married life under primitive conditions in the wilds, first in Tanganyika, then in Macedonia. She was the only white woman for miles in Tanganyika, and nearly died in a dentist's chair in Kratovo. But she recognized this for experience she could not use. No heroine of hers would ever sit in a grass hut writing a novel.

She would write only of what she knew, or could find out about. The meticulous research shows how hard she worked for the background of her eighteenth-century and Regency novels, as well as for the more serious historical ones. Aside from a few excursions to France, where she had been as a child, her early books are set largely in London and the Sussex country she knew so well. She then widened her field gradually as she came to know other parts of England. Her son went from Marlborough to Cambridge and his mother's novels follow him. And a whole new burst of country opened up for her when she and her husband started going to Scotland for his golf and toured the north of England researching the landscape and its castles for her long-projected mediaeval book. *The Quiet Gentleman*, *The Toll-Gate* and *Venetia* all have north-country backgrounds. Interestingly enough, though she and her husband spent many summers at Gullane in Scotland, and she loved the Scots, she never set a book in Scotland. Perhaps she looked on this time as pure holiday, or perhaps she sensibly blenched at Scottish dialect. She used Irishmen in *The Black Moth* and *Faro's Daughter*, and allowed herself an orgy of north-country dialect in *The Unknown Ajax*, but mostly stuck firmly to her own brand of upper- and lower-class Regency speech.

Most interesting of all is the change and development in her work over the fifty-odd years of her writing life. 'Another Georgette Heyer,' the critics used to say, with that fatal note of patronage, when each new title appeared. No wonder if it infuriated her. There is a clear line of development in her work, from the early stories of romantic adventure through the light-hearted comedy of her middle years to a warmer and graver type of book towards the end of her life. The emphasis shifts a little, too, from the dominating hero to the interesting heroine, and hero and heroine alike grow a little older with a younger couple often introduced to keep the balance. I hope to trace the thread of this development through her writing, published and unpublished, with the known facts of her life sketched in, simply, as background to her work. I think this is what that very private lady would have wished.

Chapter 1

Georgette Heyer was born on 16 August 1902, in the prosperous London suburb of Wimbledon. She was called after her father, George Heyer, who had been called after his. The original George Heyer was a Russian fur merchant who had come to England from Kharkov in the middle years of the nineteenth century, settled down and married an English girl called Alice Waters. His name, originally pronounced to rhyme with 'flyer', is obviously not Russian, but his granddaughter was emphatic, though not enthusiastic, about her Russian descent. George Heyer may have been a fugitive from the Russian pogroms of the nineteenth century. He remains an enigmatic figure, remembered by his surviving grandson as a bearded patriarch with a strong foreign accent, a love for strange words, and an alarming penchant for practical jokes.

He and his wife already had three daughters when their one son George was born in Islington in 1869. The three girls, Alice, Ilma and Inez, were all energetic and unusual women; George was to be an English gentleman. He went to King's College School in London, and then read classics at Sidney Sussex College, Cambridge, where he wrote regularly for *Granta*. But the family fortunes suffered a reverse in the 1890s and he went to teach at Weymouth College. When King's College School moved out to Wimbledon in 1897 he was invited to take over the teaching of French there. He was an immediate success, but the school had fallen on hard times, and his starting salary was only £135 a year, a miserable figure even in those days, and brought no pension rights.

Georgette Heyer with her grandmother. The sensitive child before she withdrew into her private world.

This did not prevent him from marrying Sylvia Watkins at the church of St Peter in Eltham on 10 August 1901. She was twenty-five at the time, one of the many children of a family of Thames tugboat owners. She had been an outstanding student of cello and piano at the Royal College of Music, and her surviving son remembers her as regretting her abandoned career later in life. Their one daughter, Georgette, was born almost exactly a year after the marriage. George Boris was born four years later, and Frank Dmitri five years after that. Their names are a reminder of their unusual background, but Georgette Heyer always maintained that she had no sympathy for the Russians, and their father changed the pronunciation of his name to rhyme it with 'hare' during the war years, when the Windsors and Mountbattens were doing the same sort of thing.

He was a natural and inspiring teacher, with a gift for class management, and was remembered at King's College School as 'one who has deserved well of the School'. He discovered another gift, one for fund raising, when he organized an appeal for funds for school playing fields in 1903, and he then gave up teaching. From then on, his career was a varied one. He ran the appeal for funds to move King's College Hospital from central London to Denmark Hill, organized Queen Alexandra's Charity Matinées, acted for a while as Secretary of the Memorial Theatre at Stratford and wrote occasionally for *Punch*. A Wimbledon school friend of Georgette Heyer's described her father as 'a bit of a rolling stone . . . They seemed to move about and travel a lot . . . I fancy there may have been some sort of [financial] insecurity in her childhood.' Daughter of a High Court judge herself, this friend was 'given to understand [by her family] that my friendship with Georgette was not very well thought of, but I could not have cared less . . . I loved Georgette; I thought her father delightful, he always made one laugh . . .' And Mrs Heyer was 'a pianist, closely associated with the D'Oyly Carte Co. a most charming and attractive woman'. Motherless herself, she 'envied Georgette her loving and attractive mother . . . who told me once that Georgette had the most perfect throat and vocal chords for a singer and would have a lovely contralto voice but she could hardly distinguish one note from another.' This was a disappointment to her musical mother for which literary success may never have quite compensated.

The two girls met at Miss Head's School in Wimbledon during the war, and did not make friends at first. 'She

[Georgette] had already seen a great deal of the world and a very much wider world than we in our secure little lives in Wimbledon had ever seen. She was an enigma even then; full of intelligence, a very dry caustic wit, and a tremendous sense of humour . . . We struck sparks from each other at once and were really quite bitter enemies until quite suddenly we became friends. Georgette had no friends at school other than the staff, to whom her intelligence and ability greatly appealed, but we girls in her own age group found her difficult, and I, personally, flinched from her sharp, all too accurate, caustic tongue.' But they came together over a book, *The Red Deer*, which they both liked, and 'from that moment we were friends'.

Looking back, in 1984, this friend described Georgette Heyer as a girl: 'Very good looking . . . Her hair was light brown with gold tints in it and very wavy, curling at the ends; she had most beautiful grey eyes and those strongly marked very individual eyebrows, very dark, almost black.' The friendship lasted two or three years, during which she used to spend Saturdays at the Heyer house. 'The drawing room was tacitly regarded as our private domain and there we acted play after play . . . all dialogue completely impromptu, of course, but the plots always produced by Georgette . . . I can still recognize some of the plots in her books, particularly *Beauvallet* and *The Masqueraders* and *The Black Moth*!' Georgette Heyer had already found her vocation.

The Heyer boys both went to Lancing College, and Boris, the elder and the invalid, went straight from school into a junior job with Bovril. Frank went to Cambridge (after his father's death) and became a schoolmaster, teaching for twenty-one contented years at Downside. Their sister drew a firm veil over her own education: 'I was educated at various day schools; I did not go to college. If it is of any interest, I was in Paris for some months at the beginning of the 1914–18 war . . .' Her father was working there when war broke out, and the family were living in a maisonette on the Avenue Marceau. His daughter remembered hearing the rumbling of the German gun, Big Bertha, before they returned to Wimbledon.

4

Georgette Heyer was enrolled for a while at the more socially conscious of Wimbledon's two main girls' schools, The Study, but no records of her time there survive. Neither do any of the time she spent at Miss Head's School, evidently also part of the early experience she preferred to forget. She and the one friend she made there drifted apart after the war and never met again, but the friend, regretting this, read and reread all her books: 'She lives again for me in her books . . . the wit and humour is marvellous and so completely Georgette herself. Of course she would not be satisfied with them. She was always "reaching for the sky".' Georgette Heyer was obviously close to the mark when she told her fans they could find her in her books.

One of her early novels, *Helen*, describes a father looking for the ideal education for his beloved, motherless daughter. He investigates a great many schools and decides that what they offer is worthless. They teach only grammar and facts, rather than literature and how to think. This may well be a clue to George Heyer's attitude to his daughter's education, though she went to 'various day schools' rather than having a governess like Helen, whose father was both rich and aristocratic. But, like Helen, she had a very close relationship with her father, who was undoubtedly the formative influence of her early years. 'Boys tell their Mothers,' she was later to sum it up in a letter, 'and Girls tell their Fathers.' Widely read himself, and a stimulating talker, her father encouraged her in her voracious reading and never forbade her to read anything, although he might on occasion try to discourage her.

He was away during most of the war years, having managed to obtain a captaincy in the Army Service Corps although he was over age. Later, he was in France as a requisitioning officer, where he was remembered for his 'irrepressible optimism and unfailing good temper', and by owners of *châteaux* he requisitioned as 'the persuasive English officer with the perfect French'. He was given the OBE after the war and went to work as a staff captain at the War Office but had to leave after a severe illness, and became Appeal Secretary at King's College Hospital.

The family had moved from Woodside to 11 Homefield Road, a slightly better address in Wimbledon, by 1918, and moved again in 1923 to a new house, 5 Ridgway Place, which had just been built on what had been the Ernle-Drax estate. They moved into London for a short while about this time, their frequent moves no doubt reflecting ups and downs in George Heyer's career, but the last one also probably influenced by the successful publication of *The Black Moth* in 1921. From now on, Georgette Heyer could contribute to the family's fluctuating income. The pleasant four-bedroomed house in Ridgway Place has a secluded garden running down to an old stable wall and is in easy walking distance of Wimbledon Common, the best part of the town. George Heyer had time for his literary interests. He had been invited to join the select Wimbledon Literary and Scientific Society in 1909, and renewed his membership after the war, when he gave talks on 'History in Fiction' (1923) and 'The Humour of Dickens's Minor Characters' (1925). He also translated the poems of François Villon, which the Oxford University Press published in 1924 and said they were proud to handle. His daughter appeared as Prince Arthur to his King John in a literary tableau at the Literary and Scientific Society at the tender age of eleven, and was invited to join it in 1925, but resigned on her marriage.

An important influence in her late teens was her friendship with two older girls, Joanna Cannan and Carola Oman. They both had Oxford backgrounds, having met at Wychwood School there: Carola the daughter of the historian, Sir Charles Oman, and Joanna of a member of the Oxford University Press. They were all three young women who would, these days, have automatically gone to a university and then, equally automatically, did not. They all meant to write; they all married, and they none of them let this interfere with their writing. Joanna Cannan married H. J. Pullein-Thompson in 1918 and may not have met Georgette Heyer until after this, since Carola Oman remembered their all first meeting in Wimbledon to talk books in 1919, when Georgette Heyer was seventeen, 'in a cloud of hair'. They

Georgette Heyer with her brothers Boris and Frank. She made up The Black Moth *for Boris.*

all three used their maiden names as authors. Joanna Cannan published her first novel, *The Misty Valley*, in 1922, and Carola Oman published *The Royal Road*, a romantic historical novel about Mary Queen of Scots, in 1924, two years after she married Sir Gerald Lenanton. Georgette Heyer, the youngest of the three, published *The Black Moth* in 1921 when she was nineteen.

It had begun as a serial story, told to amuse her brother Boris, who suffered from a form of haemophilia and was never very strong. When he was thirteen and his sister seventeen, just after the war, they went to Hastings for him to convalesce from a bout of illness and, she said, she made up a story 'to relieve my own boredom, and my brother's'. Their father heard some of this, thought well of it, and suggested that she prepare it for possible publication. He had had some dealings with a literary agent called Christy and arranged for her to send her manuscript to his partner, Leonard P. Moore, who promptly sold it to Constable in England and Houghton Mifflin in the United States. Published in 1921, it is still selling. In 1982 the *New York Times* gave as a crossword clue: 'She wrote *The Black Moth*.' How many other first titles of the 1920s could be used thus? The young

The tailor's visit. One of the Cruikshank illustrations for Pierce Egan's Life in London. *The hero's impeccably tailored coat and gleaming boots became clichés with Heyer imitators. Even the Black Sheep possessed 'the long-tailed coat, the knee-breeches, and the silk stockings which constituted the correct evening wear for a gentleman'.*

author had not turned against personal publicity yet. The jacket carried her picture in a central medallion.

Set in the mid-eighteenth century and obviously influenced by Baroness Orczy and Jeffery Farnol, *The Black Moth* is a young girl's wildly romantic tale, and wildly readable, but one can see why its author would not be best pleased later on, when fans insisted on preferring it to her later books. 'Death will not be your lot, my pretty one,' says Devil Andover to the girl he has abducted, and, 'For God's sake, live clean, Belmanoir,' exhorts his friend. But it is full of hints of the delights to come. Here, already, are the saturnine male lead, the marriage in danger, the extravagant wife, and the group of idle, entertaining young men. And Georgette Heyer herself liked it well enough to use the characters again, six years later, under confusingly different names, in *These Old Shades*, so titled for that very reason.

It must have been an intoxicating experience to be published at nineteen, and 'first crack out of the bag', as she herself later

8

described it. She would undoubtedly have echoed her admired Jane Austen, who, on receiving her first literary earnings, said that it only made her long for more. Mrs Heyer had some maternal qualms about her daughter's writing, but her father and her agent were enthusiastic and, apparently, uncritical. As for Georgette Heyer, she had found her vocation as a compulsive writer and the titles followed thick and fast. By the end of 1930, she had published eleven books, of which seven were experiments in various historical modes, and four the straight novels she later suppressed.

These four books are almost all the evidence there is for what her life was like in those early years, and this may be partly why she suppressed them. They do not show her genius as stylist and story-teller, but there is nothing in them of which a young author need have been ashamed and they all sold reasonably well, if significantly less so than the historical novels of the same period. The first three are about young girls growing up, the last and least successful is a brave tackling of the problem of class in English society.

In the first, *Instead of the Thorn*, published in 1923, the motherless heroine marries a brilliant author rather older than herself. Her silly father and tedious aunt blench at telling her the facts of sex before marriage, and its realities horrify her. She runs away from her remarkably forbearing husband, lives alone and learns to value marriage, and finally returns and falls in love with him. It was a bold book for an unmarried girl of twenty-one, especially in those inhibited days. But her older cousins were married, and so was Joanna Cannan, to whom the book is dedicated.

Helen, published in 1928, is the story of another motherless girl brought up to be her father's beloved companion. Entirely devoted to him, she keeps her childhood friend Richard at arms' length, but is fascinated by a dissolute young artist when she gets involved in the London smart set. Roused at first by his kisses, she recognizes overnight that the attraction is merely physical and refuses to become engaged to him. For a while, her father is companion enough for her, but when he dies suddenly she breaks down. Recovering slowly, she comes at last to value faithful, athletic Richard. He may prefer a golf course to an historical atmosphere, but he is the kind of man who can separate a pair of fighting dogs. More important, he is a reserved Englishman himself and understands the almost masculine reserve she has learned from her aristocratic father. Richard has learned something too. In the end, he comes to her not as an adorer, begging, but as a master, demanding. And she realizes that he stands for 'Love, and for friendship, and for security; she saw her future stretch before her; she thought that she had come through storm and sorrow, to a haven, and to happiness.'

That is a very forthright statement of Georgette Heyer's young view of the ideal relationship between a man and a woman, but she says very much the same thing in *Pastel*, which was published in 1929. It is the story of two sisters, shy Frances and glamorous Evelyn. Frances falls in love with brilliant young Oliver Fayre on an aristocratic country weekend, where she has suffered the agonies of the shy at a party. She thinks it is mutual, but he has hardly noticed her. Calling at their house in suburban Meldon he falls instantly in love with Evelyn and marries her. In the end, Frances settles for devoted, rugger-playing Norman and falls in love with him after marriage, while Evelyn is having a hard time with bad-tempered Oliver. Frances learns at last that: 'Men run the show and we just run the men.' She has a child and finds that: 'It is not, after all, the perfections in human nature that one loves.' Her life is bound up now in her child and her husband, 'whom she loved, and whom she hated; who was so dear yet so exasperating; who laughed with her, and suffered with her; with whom she quarrelled, and to whom she clung.'

The last of the novels, *Barren Corn*, published in 1930, is a more ambitious and a more painful book, one of Georgette Heyer's few attempts at tragedy. It opens when an English aristocrat falls disastrously in love with a beautiful young milliner, met by chance in the South of France. She says 'thank you ever so' and does frightful things with her little finger when she drinks her tea, but he marries her just the same, intending to change her. He

Georgette Heyer in the 1920s, before her marriage. Joanna Cannan's literary heroine was 'strikingly dark, and very tall . . . her eyes were beautiful . . . and she was admirably soignée'.

fails, of course, and neither can she approve of his habitual cadging on his rich relatives. In the end, convinced that she can free him in no other way, she plans and carries out a cold-blooded suicide that everyone will think an accident.

All four novels show Georgette Heyer preoccupied with the class structure of English society. *Barren Corn* is the extreme example, where the discussion is explicit, but it is the basis of all the books. Helen is an aristocrat, one of 'the' Marchants, but the other three heroines are all reduced to tongue-tied misery in a social scene with which they feel unable to cope. Elizabeth in *Instead of the Thorn* is frightened of 'smartly dressed athletic girls' while Frances in *Pastel* and Laura in *Barren Corn* are both over-whelmed by life in the English country house. Inevitably, one wonders about their creator.

The early photographs show her entrancingly pretty, with

a sensitive, open face in the 'cloud of hair' Carola Oman described. And an older cousin remembers her as 'absolutely beautiful' at this time, with such magnetism that when she appeared at a party the young men abandoned everyone else and clustered round her 'like flies round a honey-pot'. But she must have suffered from various handicaps in the competitive and stratified society of suburban Wimbledon in those socially conscious post-war years. Her background was unusual, to put it mildly. Her name sounded English enough now, but young ladies in the Twenties did not have Russian grandfathers, unless they were White Russian princes, and it seems unlikely that an ancestor on the mother's side who had brought Cleopatra's Needle up the Thames was someone to boast about either. Worst of all, Georgette was a self-confessed bluestocking, that dangerous phenomenon a female author. Was the use of a *nom de plume* for her third published book a belated attempt at concealment? If it was, it must have come too late. She had been shunned at Miss Head's School because of her sharp tongue, and probably still used unusual words, talked in sentences, and maybe even indulged in an occasional Latin tag, picked up from her father. This was not the way to attract the young male of that era, which may help to explain her mother's lack of enthusiasm for her literary ventures.

She was tall, too: five foot ten, and the fact that she was beautiful may well have been counterbalanced by the equally unconcealable fact that she was witty. Friends from every stage of her life remember her dry tongue, her elegant speech, the laughter they shared. All very well if the laughter is shared. The development from the sensitive child of the early photographs to the poised young woman of the later ones suggests some fairly drastic social experience, doubtless along the lines of what happened to her at school. Some time in her late teens or early twenties she retired behind the elegant mask.

The four novels show her with strong views about all kinds of subjects. She disliked pretentiousness in any form, and excess of any kind. She disliked bores and suffragettes; bluestockings and baby-worshippers. She said, 'Don't you get thinking this is a fair world for women, because it isn't.' She mocked jargon of every kind, psychological, literary, artistic or political. She found men more interesting than women, who either talked nothing but 'servants and the weather' or went to work and suffered from 'a magnified sense of their own importance'. She disliked free thinking and free love, and believed in self-control, good manners and form, both in life and in art. She probably agreed with Frances, in *Pastel*, that it was 'absurd to suppose that a God who loved beauty should permit ugly things to be'. She disliked snobbery but believed in a social order that associated duty with privilege. It is significant that the aristocratic hero of *Barren Corn* is as morally inferior to his wife as she is socially to him.

Behind all this runs her dominant theme of the relationship between men and women, or a man and a woman: man is logical, woman intuitive. Man therefore tends to be more interesting than woman. Helen, the most autobiographical of the four heroines, has grown up in a group of friendly young males. But it is easy to carry this kind of inference too far. Helen is athletic, shocking her middle-class aunt by riding astride, and in breeches, playing a good game of golf and of tennis. Georgette Heyer, on the other hand, took no exercise that she could avoid, stating roundly that she had no hobbies and played no ball games.

In the 1920s, she danced. And she soon found a dancing partner, the prototype, according to her brother Frank, of the reliable young men in *Helen* and *Pastel*. She met George Ronald Rougier at Christmas 1920 when both families were staying at the Bushey Park Hotel. Two years older than her, he was also taller, handsome, and in those days a tremendous talker. He took at once to George Heyer as well as to his daughter, impressed by George's wide-ranging talk, his quotations from Homer and a kind of intellectual stimulus his own family had not provided. They had sent him to Osborne and then Dartmouth, where he found his eyesight barred him from his first love, the Navy. Transferring to Marlborough, he hoped to become a barrister, but his parents

With Ronald Rougier after their wedding at St Mary's, Wimbledon, 18 August 1925, just two months after her father's death.

jibbed at the long training involved and he went instead to the Royal School of Mines to become a mining engineer.

He played first-class rugger and bridge and shared his future wife's exotic background. Slightly higher in the English social strata than the Heyers, his family were of Huguenot extraction but had settled at York, where they ran an import-export business. He himself was born and spent some time in Odessa, acquiring Russian and a passion for caviar. In the 1920s, a young woman invited to a dance was expected to bring her own partner, and he became, reliably, Georgette Heyer's, no doubt also escorting her to the theatre parties, private views and other social events she describes in the four novels. She drew a complete veil over these early years, talking of them to no one, so there is no way we can tell what else happened in her life. She could have been like her own Helen, too devoted to her father to care much about young men, or, like Frances, have met some-one who backed away, not, in her case, because she was inconspicuous, but because she was brilliant. Something must certainly have happened in her personal as well as her literary life to turn her in on herself. Growing up is drastic, but in her case it does seem to have been more so than usual.

But she still had her dancing partner. He qualified as a mining engineer in 1922 and worked for a while in Nigeria, where he read the complete *Decline and Fall of the Roman Empire*, doubtless under the influence of George Heyer. And after five years of going out with him, and watching him play rugger with the Harlequins, and presumably missing him when he was away, Georgette Heyer became engaged to him in the spring of 1925, the year her fifth novel was published. A month later, her father died suddenly of a heart attack, after playing tennis with his good friend and future son-in-law.

It must have been an appalling shock to them all. Besides the immense personal loss, it was a family disaster. George Heyer's had not been the kind of career that means security and a large pension. His wife subsided into widowhood, and from now on Georgette Heyer would be the centre of the family. Her brothers were only nineteen and fourteen when their father died. Boris was already working, but his sister would have to help put Frank through school and Cambridge. Perhaps this is partly why the beautiful, open-faced girl turned so quickly into the reserved, formidable young woman. She had professionalism thrust upon her. From now on, she would write not only because she was a compulsive writer, but because she needed the money.

Ronald was due to go prospecting in the Caucasus that autumn, and despite the sudden bereavement the wedding went ahead, very simply, with no bridesmaids and Georgette Heyer in a fashionable little cloche hat, in St Mary's Parish Church at Wimbledon on 18 August 1925, two days after her twenty-third birthday. Many years later, condoling with a similarly bereaved friend, she wrote that a girl never got over the death of her father. At the time, Ronald must have been an immense support and comfort to her.

He had found in George Heyer the friend and stimulus he needed, and the two of them could mourn him together. There is a touching passage in *Helen*, written two years later, where the heroine, also a writer, gets out her unfinished book for the first time since her father's death and finds his pencilled corrections, catching a grammatical error here, altering an inaccurate quotation there. It is hard to bear, but Helen bears it, and goes 'dry-eyed and smiling' about her business. And her faithful suitor, Richard, understands and respects this reserve.

Ronald probably did just this. They were always to be a reserved couple, aloof with strangers, warming slowly towards friends. And he was a lucky man and probably knew it. His wife was already well established as an author with what must have been a considerable, if variable, income. More important, the early novels show that she had thought a great deal about marriage and the relationship between men and women. She may not have gone into marriage passionately: she was not a passionate woman. But she most certainly went into it meaning to make it work. She learnt bridge for her husband's sake, and though she loathed any form of exercise was to spend her holidays walking round golf courses with him, unless she could find a friend to do it for her. She used to boast in later life that she had walked round more first-class golf courses than any other woman. She was one hundred per cent loyal to Ronald, said a friend, and he was entirely devoted to her. It was a very sound basis for a marriage that was to last for nearly fifty uneventful years. Happy the marriage that has no history.

Courtship had not stopped Georgette Heyer writing. Only illness, and death, would do that. *The Great Roxhythe, The Transformation of Philip Jettan* (later retitled *Powder and Patch)* and *Simon the Coldheart* were all published by 1925. They are all interesting as early experiments in the historical mode, and it is also illuminating that she later suppressed *The Great Roxhythe* and *Simon the Coldheart.* They were experiments in a direction that was not to prove propitious for her. In both of them, the central character is a man. The Great Roxhythe is Charles II's favourite, modelled on Charles I's Duke of Buckingham. Under the mask of exquisite-about-town he is secretly acting as Charles's agent in his clandestine dealings with France. Entirely devoted to his royal master, he sacrifices everything for him, and dies happy, assassinated in his service. It is probably the worst book Georgette Heyer ever wrote. The history comes awkwardly in self-conscious gobbets, the language is stilted, the plot minimal. But it is interesting in that it shows her concerned with the relations between men, rather than those between men and women, a recurrent theme in the early historical books. Roxhythe uses his mistress as cover for his secret work for Charles, but the real conflict is between his love for Charles and his friendship for his young male protégé.

Set in the reign of Henry IV, *Simon the Coldheart* is another book very largely about men and is dedicated to George Heyer, who liked it the best of his daughter's books to date. This suggests a problem she had. Should she write for women or for men? She liked men better than women, and, luckily for her, lived mostly amongst them. All through her life, she would create heroines who have lived much with men, who walk and talk like them and are admired for this by the hero. In the early books, they often dress as men too. Misogynist Simon, for instance, tells his spitfire love, who appears quite late in the book, that: 'I never knew thee until I saw thee in thy boy's clothes.' Their love-hate wooing foreshadows the later tempestuous relationships between hero and heroine and may well have pointed a way for her. There are some fine melodramatic scenes in *Simon the Coldheart*, and a good deal of stilted language. The speech of the Middle Ages always defeated Georgette Heyer.

In *The Transformation of Philip Jettan*, published by Mills & Boon in 1923, she is working her way towards her golden vein. Set in the mid-eighteenth century like *The Black Moth*, it is a love comedy of manners and misunderstandings and shows her already mistress of the lightly sketched in, convincing background. Short on plot, it is full of light-hearted comedy, and surprising people like it. Georgette Heyer herself liked it well enough to let Heinemann reprint it in 1929, when she undoubtedly needed the money, retitled *Powder and Patch*. Very significantly, she deleted the last chapter, thus totally changing

The St James's macaroni. Philip Jettan in Powder and Patch *would have looked like this after his transformation.*

the emphasis of the book, and the character of its happy ending. Philip Jettan has transformed himself into a Frenchified fop to please the woman he loves. In the first version, he wins her and takes her to Paris, to become exquisites together. In the second, they will retire to Sussex and become a country gentleman and his wife, very much like the Rougiers.

Georgette Heyer must have been writing *These Old Shades* at the time of her marriage in 1925, for it came out in 1926, during the General Strike when there were no trains, no newspapers and, of course, no advertising or reviews. An instant success, it sold 190,000 copies in hardback and established Georgette

Heyer with a public and a publisher. Heinemann had published *Simon the Coldheart* in 1925 and were to publish her historical novels for the next thirty-seven years. The instant success of *These Old Shades*, without benefit of publicity, may well have confirmed Georgette Heyer in her view that the public exposure she shrank from was unnecessary. All her life she would stay behind the mask of Mrs Ronald Rougier and get on with what she enjoyed – her writing. And her steadily successful career seems to prove her point, although it could perhaps be argued that if she had consented to make a few public appearances, to meet a critic or two, her immense personal style might have suggested to them that her books were something more than mere romantic cliché. With rare exceptions, the critics failed her throughout her life, missing the style and the humour of her work, and this may have been partly her own fault, particularly in the United States, where her success came late.

It is easy to see why *These Old Shades* was an instant success. She was a compulsive writer and it is a compulsive read. Devil Andover from *The Black Moth* has suffered a sea change into the wicked Duke of Avon (known as Satanas to his friends). An older, saturnine hero with a past, he rescues a red-haired girl in boy's clothes from the Paris gutter, sets her up as his page, finally proves her aristocratic birth and marries her. The aristocratic birth is important. If Léonie had been the bastard everyone thinks her, it would doubtless have been the Seine for her, not marriage. Even in this gripping romantic melodrama, Georgette Heyer is beginning to formulate the rules of her private world. And if Avon is the first of her Rochester-type heroes, spitfire Léonie is the ancestress of Lady Barbara Childe of *An Infamous Army* in every sense of the word.

In *These Old Shades* as in *The Transformation of Philip Jettan*, we see Georgette Heyer very much at home both at Versailles and in the Parisian salons of the mid-eighteenth century, with walking-on parts for Madame de Pompadour and Madame du Deffand, and heroes able to compose a rondeau or dominate a literary party. Georgette Heyer may not have been to a university; she had been reading instead, with immense pleasure and great profit. There is high comedy too, some riveting scenes, and a mixture of tears and laughter that she would only sometimes achieve again. But the secret of the book's instant and lasting success lies in its sheer romantic gusto. She was writing with an easy pen that first year of her marriage.

Conditions in the Caucasus, where Ronald went to work two months after their marriage, were impossible for a woman, and his wife stayed at home in the flat they had taken at Earls Court, doubtless helping her mother with the slow and painful adjustment to widowhood. Mrs Heyer made no attempt to revive her music, but dwindled into a hotel life that was to last for almost forty years. Georgette Heyer must have been missing her father just as much. She describes her Helen as unable to write for some time after her father's death, but Helen is an aristocrat, and rich; she does not have to write for a living. Her own case was very different. From now on, she would undoubtedly have subscribed to Dr Johnson's dictum that no one but a fool ever wrote save for money. She would later say that she could not write under stress, but in her twenties she managed it. It is true that she published no book in 1927, but she made up for this amply in the following years, publishing *Helen* and *The Masqueraders* in 1928, *Beauvallet* and *Pastel* in 1929, *Barren Corn* in 1930 and *The Conqueror* in 1931.

Ronald was back in England by the summer of 1926, but went to Tanganyika that autumn. His wife joined him there in the spring of 1927 and lived in a compound in the bush, surrounded by lions and leopards and rhinoceroses. It must have been an extraordinary experience for the girl who had grown up in Wimbledon, and an acid test of their marriage. There was one other white man, a rough Cornish miner, in their compound. Aside from him, the nearest white people were a hundred and fifty miles away. Their native servants had never seen a white woman before, and she was left alone with them for long spells while her husband was on safari, prospecting for tin. She went too, just once, travelling twenty rough miles a day, on a strict allowance of one water bottle. She did not complain, but she did not go again. She

The Dandy Club. Georgette Heyer's notebooks contain a page of cravats tied in Oriental, Mathematical, Osbaldeston, Napoleon, American, Mailcoach (or Waterfall) styles.

wrote an article about the rhinoceros for the *Sphere* in 1929: 'It is not wise to despise the rhino . . . The first time I saw one of these grotesque beasts I felt considerably scared, but as time went on I became a little *blasé* about them. Familiarity breeds contempt.'

She wrote *The Masqueraders* in Tanganyika, taking another step into what was to be her private world. It is a curiously uneven book, set just after Bonnie Prince Charlie's disastrous rising of 1745. Dangerously involved in this by their adventurer father, the hero and heroine change roles. Tall Prudence dresses as a man, slight Robin as a girl. They have done it before in their ramshackle career, and are soon established in London society and plunged into the inevitable comic-romantic imbroglio, courting across the sexes. It all ends happily when their father turns out to be not the pretender he pretends, but the real Lord Barham. Once again, it is necessary to be an aristocrat. Writing in the bush, Georgette Heyer got one fact wrong, the date of the founding of White's Club, by one year. The book is romantic, sometimes moving, always highly entertaining, but marred by its slightly stilted language, its tendency to 'egad' and 'ecod'.

By the time it was published in 1928, Ronald Rougier was prospecting in Macedonia, where his wife joined him. She nearly died of an erratically administered anaesthetic in a dentist's chair in Kratovo, lived in a haunted house, she said, and wrote *Pastel* there, dedicating it to her mother. The climax of this book is when Frances has her baby daughter and feels that she is even at last with her brilliant older sister, or rather that their rivalry no longer matters. It shows which way Georgette Heyer's mind was working: she wanted to have a child. Macedonia was Ronald's last prospecting job. He had never really wanted to be a mining engineer and had not been a particularly successful one. They decided to come back to England, where he would look about him while she supported them by her writing, something that *These Old Shades* had proved to be entirely possible.

They were back in London by 1929 and Ronald ventured into a brief, unlucky partnership in a gas, light and coke company in the Horseferry Road. If his future seemed uncertain, his wife's was quite otherwise. She had tried five different English publishers by now and had found one that really suited her. All her life, she would need and want a close personal relationship with her publisher, and she found this at Heinemann, whose young managing director, A. S. Frere, was to become a lifelong friend, counsellor and confidant. He himself, at this time, was still deeply involved in his passionate friendship with another author who preferred anonymity, Lady Russell, who had been best-selling as Elizabeth of the German Garden since 1898. He probably had more sense than to let the two formidable ladies meet. He remembers Georgette Heyer as being discouraged when they first met over the publication of *Simon the Coldheart* in 1925, feeling that she had made no progress. The phenomenal success of *These Old Shades* next year changed all this and encouraged Heinemann to take over the rights in her previous books, reprinting *The Great Roxhythe* and *The Black Moth* in 1929, and *The Transformation of Philip Jettan* as *Powder and Patch* in 1930.

They also published a new historical novel, *Beauvallet*, in 1929. Dedicated to her brother Frank, it is set in the reign of Queen

Elizabeth, another of her swashbuckling stories centred round the hero. It is written with considerable speed and certainty: 'The fight was desperate over the slippery decks: sword to sword, slash and cut, and the quick stab of daggers.' There is some good detail, plenty of stilted language and a rather routine romantic plot, but it sold 86,000 copies and helped to consolidate her position as an author whose historical novels would sell themselves. A. S. Frere was later to sum it up: the only problem with her was whether to print sixty, eighty, or a hundred and twenty thousand copies.

Ronald's life was going less well. The partnership had been a disaster, and lost them money. They heard of a sports shop in Horsham, borrowed some money from Mrs Heyer's sisters, which was repaid, with interest, over the years, and moved down to Sussex. Boris Heyer, who had persuaded his mother to let him throw up his safe, dull job with Bovril, was out of work and would live over the shop and help Ronald run it, while Georgette ran the house and wrote the books that were their security. They found a rambling, two-storeyed comfortable house called Southover in the tiny hamlet of Colegate at Lower Beeding, a few miles from Horsham. It was in deep country, approached by what must have been an extremely muddy lane in winter, but the four-bedroomed house was pleasant, oddly similar in general layout to 5 Ridgway Place, and had a big living room and secluded views down to a lake. Ronald commuted into Horsham to string tennis racquets and repair guns, learning to charge at least seven shillings and sixpence for any job or the customer would not be satisfied. It was just as well that Heinemann were reprinting Georgette Heyer's old titles.

Her friend Joanna Cannan published a novel called *No Walls of Jasper* in 1930 and dedicated it to Georgette Heyer. It contains a description of a lady authoress that may well have been taken from the life:

Cynthia Bechler was a historical novelist; her 'cloak and sword' romances were nearer to 'best sellers' than anything to be found in the sober general catalogue of Messrs. Curtis, Fayre and Haydon. She was dark; not just brown-haired . . . but strikingly dark, and very tall; fifty years ago she would have been ridiculed as a 'maypole' and considered unmarriageable. She was not beautiful, not pretty; her nose was too large, aquiline yet lacking delicacy, and she had too full a mouth, too heavy a chin. But her eyes were beautiful, almond-shaped, tawny amber-brown, the lower, as well as the upper, lashes prettily curled; and she was admirably *soignée* . . .

Unfortunately there is no record of whether Georgette Heyer recognized the likeness. She was busy with a project close to her heart at this time. This was *The Conqueror*, which Heinemann published in 1931. It is another book with the hero as centre of the action but an immense advance on the previous ones. Significantly, she dedicated it to her good friend Carola Oman, now established as a successful historical writer: 'In friendship and in appreciation of her own incomparable work done in the historical manner dear to us both.' This book about William the Conqueror was to be a serious venture into historical biography, and she researched it thoroughly. It was an easy matter to cross from Newhaven to Dieppe and explore the Normandy countryside, and she had joined the London Library in 1928 and was now able to take advantage of the country member's allowance of fifteen books at a time, which the invaluable library would post down to her. Many years later she wrote to an American reviewer about *The Conqueror*: 'It wasn't until I read your letter that I remembered what a lot of work I put into it! And how difficult it was to correlate the various contemporary (and largely inaccurate) accounts of William's Life and Times – a Task not made easier by the fact that, at that date, hardly anyone had a surname, and that the Chronicles bestowed Christian names in a somewhat haphazard way, Ralph de Toeni, for instance, appearing, indifferently, as Ralph, Raoul, Reynaud, and Richard! And, even worse, that awful Fitz, meaning "the son of". All very well if the character was historic-

Walking costume, 1800.

ally important, or if his father had an unusual name, such as Osbern; but although any student of the period knows All About William Fitzosbern, few could be expected to recognize William Fitzwilliam as his son. Well, not at a *glance*, anyway!'

The Conqueror is the story of William from his bastard birth to his crowning as King of England. Georgette Heyer allowed herself some latitude in telling it, having enriched William's life with a close man friend, Raoul de Harcourt, and a Shakespearian jester, Galet, very much in the vein of the fool in

King Lear. One should never forget that the Rougier family played Shakespearian games in the evening, and it is a measure of Georgette Heyer's awareness of what would and would not do in her kind of book that her Shakespearian echoes are so comparatively few.

The Conqueror shows her very much mistress of military strategy, with William's swift marches and brilliant siege technique brought vividly to life. She makes the most of his violent wooing of Matilda, daughter of Count Baldwin of Flanders, whom he whips publicly. It is a fantastic scene, for which there is some historical justification in J. H. Planché's *The Conqueror and his Companions*, which is still available on the shelves of the London Library. The rough wooing ends in happy marriage. William is the master. Raoul, in a useful sub-plot, has fallen in love with Elfrida, sister of his Saxon hostage friend Edgar. In the end, after Hastings, he will be master of her and of dead Edgar's estates in England. There is no question where Georgette Heyer's sympathies lie. They are with the men, and the Normans. Apart from Edgar, who becomes civilized by long and honourable captivity at William's court, the Saxons are barbarians, the Normans the people with manners. Mocking Saxon witchcraft, Georgette Heyer reveals what was to be a weakness in her serious historical work. Religion as a mainspring of human behaviour simply did not exist for her. When Harold swears on the reliquaries and then breaks his oath, the question is of man's betrayal of man; God does not enter into it. Religion and the part it plays in human affairs was one of the things Georgette Heyer chose to leave out of her books. Less important in the eighteenth-century and Regency novels, this is a fatal lack in the books set earlier.

The Conqueror was turned down in the United States, where her publishing career had been as varied as in England. She moved from Houghton Mifflin, who had published *The Black Moth*, to Small Maynard (also of Boston) with *The Great Roxhythe* (1923). They then turned down *The Transformation of Philip Jettan*, but published *Instead of the Thorn* (1924), *Simon the Coldheart* (1925), and

These Old Shades (1926). But they turned down *Helen*, which came out from Longman on both sides of the Atlantic, and Longman then published her steadily in the United States until they rejected *The Conqueror*. This left her without an American publisher until Doubleday took *Death in the Stocks* and published it as *Merely Murder* in 1935. A woman who rode her prejudices like hobby-horses, she indulged in one against the Americans, which always broke down when she met a sympathetic individual one. But she never considered going there, and never let the American market enter into her professional calculations. A sale there was a bonus, no more.

She herself described *The Conqueror*, forty years later, as 'not amongst my best sellers'. Turned down in America, it sold fewer copies than *The Masqueraders* and less than half those of *These Old Shades* in England. She drew her own conclusions. She hardly ever talked about her past, but she did, just occasionally, speak of the grinding financial anxiety of those years in Sussex. In 1931, planning ahead, she decided to channel her creative gift in a more prosperous direction.

Chapter 2

1932 was a crucial year in Georgette Heyer's life. Her first thriller, *Footsteps in the Dark*, came out from Longman, who had published her straight novels, while Heinemann published the last and strongest of her early historical romances, *Devil's Cub*. Infinitely more important in her view was the birth of Richard George Rougier whom she was later to describe as 'my most notable (indeed peerless) work', and 'my most successful achievement'. It was an easy birth: 'I saw my quite ordinary G.P. *twice* before he came to deliver me, and produced a Fine, healthy male child without the least trouble.' In an unpublished essay on 'Fathers' she said: 'No one is going to persuade Father that she enjoyed almost the whole performance, and forgot within a matter of minutes any stage of it that wasn't wholly delightful.'

She was a devoted mother, but she was also the major wage earner of both the Rougier and the Heyer families. By the time her brother Frank had left Cambridge and gone to work as a teacher, it must have been evident that Boris would always need a certain amount of help, and so would their mother, to whom Georgette Heyer was to make over the foreign rights of her books, with the exception of the American ones. Ronald's future, too, must have seemed quite uncertain at this time. It is not surprising that Richard remained an only and sometimes a lonely child. They moved, soon after his birth, to another pleasant, secluded country house not far from Horsham. This was Blackthorns, Toad Hill, Slinfold, a rather larger house which they altered considerably, extending the living room and adding

Georgette Heyer with Richard, 1933. She wrote that Footsteps in the Dark *was 'published simultaneously with my son on 12 February 1932'.*

a steep back stair from kitchen to attic bedrooms so that they could have living-in servants. This does not imply any great level of affluence. In those days every middle-class family had at least one daily maid. The Rougiers certainly had more. A friend who stayed with them at Blackthorns remembers neither domestic duties nor the constant presence of Richard. When she did the flowers for her hostess, who disliked the job, the old ones, left in the pantry, just vanished. It was a comfortable house, well staffed and well run, and, inevitably, expensive. It is no wonder that Georgette Heyer was aiming to write one historical and one detective novel a year.

Blackthorns is set back down its own drive from what must then have been a quiet country lane and stands in considerable gardens and grounds sloping away to woods where the nightingales sang so loudly that people came from London to hear them. Deer still wander into the garden to eat the young plants, and there is still no other house in sight. There was room for the Irish wolfhound, the bull terrier and the Siamese cat that was its friend and had to share living space with it when they were put in kennels. Toad Hill is now Toat Hill, but when the present owners bought the house the postman remembered it as Georgette Heyer's. The old lady who lived at the end of the drive remembers Richard as a lonely little boy who would come and see her and tell her that Mummy was busy writing. His father would drop in and pick him up on his way home from work. His grandmother, Mrs Heyer, had moved to Horsham and she, too, was apt to complain that her daughter was always busy.

It was hardly surprising. Those were the years of the Depression, and it is unlikely that a sports shop run by a couple of unbusinesslike amateurs in a small English market town would go anywhere near supporting three adults and a baby. And Ronald Rougier's heart cannot have been entirely in the shop. Encouraged by his wife, he was already working towards the career he had always wanted, that of a barrister. At about this time, the athletic heroes of Georgette Heyer's novels were being replaced by the elegant young solicitors and barristers who appear so frequently in her detective stories.

These were a new departure. Georgette Heyer was thirty in 1932. She had been published for eleven years, by five English publishers and three American ones, and must have been thinking hard about where her future lay. *Barren Corn* had sold significantly less well than the three other straight novels and she seems to have regarded that direction as closed. There were probably more reasons for this than the financial one. It had been all very well to write *Pastel* in Macedonia and set it in 'Meldon', a suburb obviously based on her own memories of Wimbledon. Absence is very liberating. Now she was living for the first time deep in the English countryside and learning what an exposed business this is. She herself said that she 'played no ball games and belonged to no clubs'. So how did she find English country life?

Doubtless by her choice, neither of their two country houses was actually in a village, so she was not immediately exposed to the strong corporate eye of the small community, but she must have been very much aware of it. Servants come and go, and talk. The detective stories she wrote in the Thirties show her intensely conscious of the strong roots of gossip that run under any village. She may not have joined the Women's Institute or gone to the parish church, but the postman knew who she was just the same. If she wrote another modern novel, the neighbours would read it, and draw their conclusions.

Footsteps in the Dark, written when she was pregnant with Richard, was an experiment in a new field, the thriller. She later described it as 'in the Wallace style' and 'not up to much'. It is set in a Sussex village where a group of young people move into an old house that has long stood empty. It has panelled rooms, rambling cellars, and a rumoured ghost, and turns out to be riddled with secret passages. There is a lively feeling of village life and some quickly sketched characters: the entomologist, the inebriate doctor, the white-gloved vicar's wife whom nobody loves. The plot is simple enough. The house is the headquarters of a gang of forgers, and their leader is trying to frighten the young people away by the apparent haunting that begins with footsteps in the dark and works up to abduction and murder. There is a powerful-looking young man who behaves suspiciously, falls in love with the heroine, and turns out to be a policeman in disguise. It is not entirely convincing, but enormous fun, and merits a reprint. Though it was published by Longman, who had done the straight novels, these are not listed as previous titles, so she must have already decided to suppress them. Its first printing of 5,000 equalled the total sales of *Barren Corn* and another 11,000 copies had been printed by 1936. This was encouraging enough that she continued to explore the new vein, publishing nine more mystery stories in the next nine years.

The early Thirties were a good time to be trying one's hand in the field of mystery. The novel was in its usual state of twentieth-century disarray, with Proust and Joyce in the ascendant and Virginia Woolf far out in *The Waves* (1931). People who wanted to write good old-fashioned tales (and make some money by them) were increasingly taking refuge in the detective story and the straight thriller. In them, moral standards and a happy ending were not just tolerated but expected, and in those days they had not succumbed to the twin modern curses of sex and violence. Margery Allingham describes the situation in a preface to a later omnibus volume, *The Mysterious Mr Campion*. Mystery writers in the late Twenties and early Thirties were refugees, she says, from a world in emotional chaos. 'We have the privilege of Court Fools. There is very little we dare not say in any company in the land. Nobody honours us . . . for blurting out the truth if it occurs to us; but then . . . nobody stops us.' An interesting group of women were taking advantage of this freedom. Agatha Christie was well established; Margery Allingham, Dorothy Sayers, Ngaio Marsh and Patricia Wentworth were all beginning their immensely successful careers. Where Edgar Wallace had made the mystery story popular, they were making it respectable.

The historical romance, on the other hand, was still in the critical doldrums, but it went on selling. *Devil's Cub*, published in the same year as *Footsteps in the Dark*, had a printing of 115,000 copies as against 16,000 for *Footsteps in the Dark*. It is at once the last of Georgette Heyer's early swashbuckling romances and the first of her books where comedy of manners is almost as important as story. And it shows an interesting development in her attitude to the main theme of her historical romance, the relationship between men and women. It is the story of the Duke of Avon's rakehell son Dominic Vidal, who meets his match when he abducts Mary Challoner in mistake for her complaisant sister. One of Georgette Heyer's first scenes of high dramatic comedy follows. Drunk and furious, Vidal turns on Mary:

'You've thrown yourself at my head, and by God I'll take you . . .'

He was advancing towards her. She brought her right hand from behind her, and levelled the pistol. 'Stand where you are,' she said. 'If you come one step nearer I shall shoot you down.'

He stopped short. 'Where did you get that thing?' he demanded.

'Out of your coach,' she answered.

'Is it loaded?'

'I don't know,' said Miss Challoner, incurably truthful.

He began to laugh again, and walked forward. 'Shoot then,' he invited, 'and we shall know. For I'm coming several steps nearer, my lady.'

Miss Challoner saw that he meant it, shut her eyes and resolutely pulled the trigger. There was a deafening report and the Marquis went staggering back. He recovered in a moment. 'It was loaded,' he said coolly.

By the time Mary has bound up his wound, put him to bed, and sent for the doctor, it is clear enough how the story is to end, but Georgette Heyer keeps the tension high for another two-thirds of the book. Vidal has compromised Mary and feels he must marry her: she will not have him on those terms. Besides, she is below him in rank. Her father married a vulgar woman. To free him, she elopes at last with his cousin's pompous lover and learns, as many other Georgette Heyer heroines are to do, what a dull prig a romantically-minded young man can be. And he is shocked by her, poor man: 'A natural female agitation would have given his chivalry more scope, but Miss Challoner remained maddeningly calm, and, far from betraying weakness or nervous fears, assumed the direction of the journey.' When Mary marries Vidal at last, it will be the marriage of equals in every sense. Because Mary, like her future mother-in-law, Léonie, of *These Old Shades*, is socially saved by the possession of a highly respected general by way of grandfather. This is Georgette Heyer's private world, with its private rules, and birth is important.

The contrast in the sales of *Footsteps in the Dark* and *Devil's Cub* must have been a serious consideration for someone who was the financial centre of her extended family, but detective stories made a change, and, besides, they were something that Ronald enjoyed. A friend remembers him at this time as an immensely supportive husband, charming, friendly and always there when his wife needed him, if perhaps always a step behind. And he was a tower of strength when it came to reading proofs, where she relied on him to catch errors she was too close to spot. But he actually collaborated in the detective stories. For the next ten years or so, she would write one detective story and one romantic historical novel a year, and he would provide the plots for the detective stories. He worked them out in terms of lay figures described as A, B and C. She then gave the characters life and relationships, complaining from time to time that A or B just would not behave like that. It must have been an enormously entertaining way to pass a quiet country evening when he came home from work. And when he began to read for the Bar a whole new world of professional expertise opened up for them both.

She later described the way they worked: 'I do these things with the assistance – and ONLY with the assistance of G. R. Rougier . . . [he] still dines out on his version of what happened over *No Wind of Blame*, which was a highly technical shooting mystery . . . I DID know, broadly speaking, how the murder was committed, but I didn't clutter up my mind with the incomprehensible details. Ronald swears that he came home one evening when I was at work on the final, explanatory chapter

Evening dress, 1800.

and that I said to him: "If you're not too busy, could you tell me just how this murder was committed?"'

She might well ask. It remains, unfortunately, incomprehensible to the average reader. Collaborations are risky. When two minds run together, they must go at the pace of the slower one.

Georgette Heyer was intensely, instinctively creative. Ronald was rational, analytic, and obstinate. Harnessed to his plots, however technically sound, her genius was inhibited, and it showed. There is a failure of homogeneity in these books, with character too visibly giving way to plot. She was later to say that: '*Why Shoot a Butler?* is so complicated it baffles *me*.' In this connection, it is interesting to bear in mind that throughout her life, Ronald was always his wife's first reader. It was his chuckles as he read it that reassured her that all was well with her latest book.

Why Shoot a Butler? came out in 1933 and *The Unfinished Clue* in 1934, both from Longman. *Why Shoot a Butler?* is an old-fashioned, romantic thriller about murder and a missing will, and *The Unfinished Clue* is a thoroughly good country house mystery with an intricate plot based on timing, a romantic interest for the gentleman detective, and what Georgette Heyer herself later described as 'a superb lady called Lola'. She described *Death in the Stocks*, published in 1935, as: 'The first of what I call my *real* crime stories.' It introduced two detectives she was to use again, Superintendent Hannasyde and Sergeant Hemingway, but though she worked hard at giving them character, making Hemingway a dabbler in psychology, they never achieved the popularity of Poirot, or Alleyn, or Peter Wimsey. In fact, two of the best of her detective stories have gentleman sleuths. In *The Unfinished Clue* she tried her hand at a gentleman police inspector who falls in love with the heroine, reveals that he has always really wanted to be a barrister, and resigns from the force. In *Death in the Stocks*, though Hannasyde is in charge of the case, it is solved by Giles Carrington, the solicitor hero. The best things in this book are the scenes of light-hearted comedy among the young people and the engaging young solicitor hero, recognizable at once by his 'pleasant, lazy voice'.

Georgette Heyer moved to Hodder & Stoughton with her fifth detective story, *Behold, Here's Poison*, perhaps because she was dissatisfied with Longman's printing of only 5,000 for *Death in the Stocks*, the same number as for *The Unfinished Clue*, and fewer than for *Why Shoot a Butler?* Hodder then published four more detective stories, all featuring Hannasyde or Hemingway or both. They are all set in the English scene she knew, in large country houses or prosperous suburban ones. They have good scenes and entertaining characters like the religious maniac policeman who turns out to be the murderer, and a fine gallery of elderly ladies with some pointed dialogue to remind us that she was an avid reader of Ivy Compton-Burnett as well as of Jane Austen. But her ear for modern speech was not so infallible as it was to prove for her own Regency dialogue. The books were referred to in the family as pot boilers, and from time to time this shows, as when she allows a character to talk about 'wending thitherwards'. And, as she herself was to point out later, the advantage of historical writing is that its slang cannot date. People did say 'jumping Jehosophat', and 'it isn't at all the clean potato', in the early 1930s, but it is hard to believe it now.

The detective stories were treated with respect at the time, and all of them except *Footsteps in the Dark* are still in print. Georgette Heyer was hailed as Queen of Mystery and Suspense, and *Death in the Stocks*, for instance, was reviewed by both *The Times* and the *Times Literary Supplement*, which called it 'an excellent example of what can be achieved when the commonplace material of detective fiction is worked up by an experienced novelist.' *The Times* crossword puzzle gave 'author of *Envious Casca*' as a clue, and *Death in the Stocks* was dramatized, but ran for only three nights in New York.

Georgette Heyer herself summed up the position when she wrote later that 'my thrillers are not my main source of income, and never will be.' She continued to average two books a year while Richard was growing up and Ronald dividing his time between the sports shop, his reading for the Bar and his collaboration in the detective stories. As well as writing hard, his wife was reading immensely. They had a settled home now, and some space, and she was beginning to collect her reference library and to accumulate the research material that gives so much of its character to her work. Illustrations from magazine articles were lovingly clipped and filed, so that she could turn up pictures of six different neckcloths or six different bonnets as required. Useful material from books was carefully traced or copied to provide pages of carriages, or furniture or uniforms. She had pictures of prominent people, from George IV in his coronation robes to unattributed Gainsboroughs. Avidly collecting, she did not trouble to record where the clips came from, or, often, their subjects. It was enough that she had them.

She was collecting books, too. Second-hand books were cheap and plentiful in those days, and the London Library a rich source of material about the late eighteenth and early nineteenth centuries. She probably found Pierce Egan's *Life in London* there. This lively contemporary description of the goings-on of a couple of young men about town during the Regency was brilliantly illustrated by Cruikshank with scenes at Almack's, Tattersall's, Covent Garden and so on, and was one of her first goldmines of Regency slang. She soon bought her own two-volume edition, elegant leather-bound volumes which she would lovingly polish from time to time along with the rest of her old books.

She only published one book, *Why Shoot a Butler?*, in 1933, which probably reflects both the first year of Richard's life and a great deal of time spent on research. The next three historical novels, *The Convenient Marriage* (1934), *Regency Buck* (1935), and *The Talisman Ring* (1936), show her very much at home in the private world she was making her own. The meticulous files of notes on language and people and customs of the late eighteenth and early nineteenth centuries had been growing fast. She could turn to her indexed vocabulary books and find *rumbo* for Newgate when she wanted to introduce thieves' cant in *The Convenient Marriage*, or a Bow Street Runner in *The Talisman Ring*. The first entry under 'Police' in the vocabulary books is a *bum-trap*, actually identified as from Egan, but mostly she gives no sources and very few dates for her lovingly collected words and phrases. Under 'Abuse, Male', *shagbag* meaning contemptible is dated as 1740, *codger* for mean, as 1760; and *ugly customer*, as 1811; while *hen-of-the-game* for shrew under 'Abuse, Female' is dated 1589,

A page of uniforms from one of the Regency notebooks. Georgette Heyer knew exactly what her military heroes wore.

showing how widely she cast her net. But mostly she must have relied on her own instinct to decide between *scrub*, *snabster*, *snipper-snapper* and *snirp* when she needed a bit of male abuse.

She had also been collecting background detail about the minutiae of Regency life, and could turn to her files for notes and illustrations of every aspect of it from 'Banks' to 'Women'. In fact, elated with her own research, she introduced almost too much detail of journeys and furniture into *Regency Buck*, but came out strong with the Brighton road when Judith Taverner shocked her world by racing her curricle down it, or a cockfight at which her brother Peregrine could get into trouble. And when she wanted a Royal Prince to fall in love with Judith, there was the Duke of Clarence, ready in her notes, with his famous remark about the Thames: 'There it goes, flow, flow, flow, always the same.' She devoted almost two pages to the Pavilion at Brighton, which makes her heroine feel faint, and no wonder. Always her own most acute critic, she would not use quite so much background detail again, until it began to creep back in during the last years of her life. These three books are immensely significant for the development of her own inimitable (if too often imitated) kind of book – 'the Georgette Heyer'. Each of them still has some of the thriller elements of the earlier historical novels, most pronounced in *The Talisman Ring*, which is very nearly a detective story in period costume, but each of them also glows with the kind of stylish romantic comedy that was to be her hallmark. In *The Convenient Marriage*, Lord Rule has proposed to the eldest Miss Winwood, but has let her younger sister, Horry, persuade him to marry her instead. His sister calls on him, and learns of this:

'Marcus, is the girl a minx?' she asked.

'No,' he answered. 'She is not, Louisa. I am not at all sure that she is not a heroine.'

'Don't she wish to marry you?'

The Earl's eyes gleamed. 'Well, I am rather old, you know, though no one would think it to look at me. But she assures me she would quite like to marry me. If my memory serves me, she prophesied that we should deal famously together.'

Lady Louisa, watching him, said abruptly: 'Rule, is this a love-match?'

His brows rose; he looked faintly amused. 'My dear Louisa! At my age?'

'Then marry the Beauty,' she said. 'That one would understand better.'

'You are mistaken, my dear. Horatia understands perfectly. She engages not to interfere with me.'

'At seventeen! It's folly, Marcus.' She got up, drawing her scarf around her. 'I'll see her for myself.'

'Do,' he said cordially. 'I think – but I may be prejudiced – you will find her adorable.'

'If you find her so,' she said, her eyes softening, 'I shall love her – even though she has a squint!'

'Not a squint,' said his lordship. 'A stammer.'

This is the first of the historical novels that begins with the marriage of the protagonists and ends with their reaching an understanding at last. This raises, at once, the distinction Georgette Heyer makes between love and sex. Careful reading reveals that Rule has, in fact, slept with his Horry, and has begun to neglect her as misunderstanding grows between them. He is in love with her; she will learn to love him, just like the heroine of *Instead of the Thorn*. But sex is something that happens off-stage and is kept in its place. It is important, never all-important. It is the marriage of two minds that matters most to Georgette Heyer, not four bare legs in a bed, and this is one of the reasons for her lasting success. Attitudes to sex change from generation to generation and changed drastically during her lifetime, but she had chosen her line and kept to it. Her son, many years later, described her, to her amusement, as 'not so much square as cubed', and she made a revealing remark about his upbringing. 'Your morals are your own affair,' she used to tell him, 'but your manners are mine.' But in her private world, manners and morals were almost the same thing, and equally important. In these days of compulsory sex in the novel, one turns with relief to the manners and morals of Georgette Heyer's private world.

Manners, of course, imply class, which had always been a preoccupation of hers. There is, perhaps inevitably, an element of snobbery in the four modern novels and the detective stories, just as there is in the detective stories of her contemporaries, with their gentleman detectives, their Lord Peter Wimsey and Roderick Alleyn. She must have recognized this problem at an early stage and solved it brilliantly by retreating into her private Regency world, which had snobbery built in, historical, and therefore respectable. We are all snobs of some kind, and it is comfortable to find oneself in a world where the rules are so clearly established, where privilege and duty go hand in hand,

and a terrible mockery awaits anyone who takes advantage of position. This is a world, like that of Shakespeare's comedies, where laughter is the touchstone and the purifier; where exposure to the mockery of one's equals is punishment enough equally for Montagu Revesby in *Friday's Child* or Parolles in *All's Well that Ends Well.*

If *The Convenient Marriage* is the first of the books that begins with the marriage of hero and heroine, *Regency Buck* is the first that is concerned with the merry war between upstanding heroine and enigmatic hero. Its main plot is slight, but it has a lively detective-style sub-plot. Georgette Heyer once said that her style was a blend of Dr Johnson and Jane Austen and this book shows her perhaps, if this is possible, too heavily influenced by Jane Austen, whose neat ironic style sits oddly with a melodramatic plot. Judith Taverner is actually reading *Sense and Sensibility* and quotes it to Worth. Georgette Heyer herself was more likely reading *Mansfield Park.* 'There is a volatility, a habit of being too generally pleasing which must preclude my taking him in any very serious spirit,' says Judith of Captain Audley, sounding disconcertingly like Fanny Price.

Like *Regency Buck*, *The Talisman Ring* is set mainly in Sussex, Georgette Heyer's home ground at the time. It is a light-hearted romp through known country, with a vivacious French heroine rather giving way to a powerful English one. Eustacie has rejected Sir Tristram because he is not the kind of man who would ride *ventre à terre* to her death-bed. At the end of the book:

> Eustacie, finding her tongue, blurted out: 'But, Sarah, do you *want* to marry Tristram?'
>
> Miss Thane's eyes twinkled. 'My love, when a female reaches my advanced years, she cannot be picking and choosing, you know. She must be content with the first respectable offer she receives.'
>
> . . . 'But, Sarah, consider! You are romantic, and he is not romantic at all!'

'I know,' replied Miss Thane, 'but I assure you I mean to come to an understanding with him before the knot is tied . . . Either I have his solemn promise to ride *ventre à terre* to my death-bed or there will be no marriage!'

'It shall be included in the marriage vow,' said Sir Tristram.

Eustacie, looking from one to the other, made a discovery. '*Mon Dieu*, it is not a *mariage de convenance* at all! You are in love, *enfin*!' she exclaimed.

'Romantic I am not,' Georgette Heyer once said, and this scene provides a useful gloss to the statement. It all depends what you mean by romantic. While she was writing the neat comedy of *The Talisman Ring* she was deep in her notebooks. Three serious, solidly researched historical novels were to follow it: *An Infamous Army* in 1937, *Royal Escape* in 1938 and *The Spanish Bride* in 1940. Her notes for all of them survive, written in her neat longhand and carefully bound together with green ribbon. They represent formidable weeks of research. She said herself that she had covered every one of the many contemporary sources for the Battle of Waterloo, the climax of *An Infamous Army*, and the notes are there to confirm this, meticulously cross-referred. Complete with their own bibliographies, the notes for each book are illustrated with careful sketches of uniforms and hand-drawn maps, of Waterloo, for instance, for *An Infamous Army*, and of Badajoz, where the story of *The Spanish Bride* opens.

It is fascinating to turn from the notes to the books themselves and see at once her passionate accuracy, and the genius with which she could breathe life into the hard, historical fact. *An Infamous Army* sets a strong romantic story in Brussels during the weeks leading up to Waterloo. Her description of the climactic battle has been used at Sandhurst and acclaimed as the best there is, and her son remembers the only public lecture she ever gave. She took him, as a schoolboy, to the United Services Institute, where they found a model of the battle, and she began to describe it to him, too absorbed to notice the arrival of a bevy of schoolgirls, whose attendant mistress recognized the expert and told them to hush and listen to her. Characteristically, hearing this, Georgette Heyer hushed herself, and moved away.

Many people, including her family, think *An Infamous Army* Georgette Heyer's best book. Her friend and publisher A. S. Frere remembers her own enthusiasm for it. 'I am going to hang it round your neck,' she told him. She gave it an extra richness by rooting it deep in her own earlier work. The heroine, Lady Barbara Childe, is granddaughter to the Devil's cub, Dominic Vidal, and his Mary, who appear at the end of the book. And the hero is Charles Audley who had a lively walking-on part in *Regency Buck* and was dismissed by the heroine as volatile. He has settled down now as a popular member of Wellington's staff but falls headlong in love with bad Lady Barbara, who owes a good deal to Lady Caroline Lamb of the tempestuous affairs and damped muslins. Lady Barbara's relationship with Audley is enlivened by a brief passage between her and young Peregrine Taverner, also from *Regency Buck*.

Georgette Heyer made a point of not re-reading *Vanity Fair* while she was writing *An Infamous Army*, and when she did turn to it afterwards she was shocked at Thackeray's lack of research as revealed in his assumption that the gunfire of the battle could be heard in Brussels. She had read all the contemporary diaries and letters about the battle and knew that no firing was heard there all day. Her own book, based on this intensive research, is her most ambitious and one of her most successful projects. Her portrait of the Duke of Wellington, based on his own letters and reported speech, is masterly. 'I've done Wellington a fair treat,' she wrote Frere. 'He simply slipped out of my pen on to the paper. I can't tell you how many books I have read dealing with him!' She loved Wellington and even went to the trouble of securing an actual letter of his, so when she describes his boldly flowing pen she knows just what she is talking about. And the climax of the book shows her writing at her lucid best for over a hundred pages, from the time when the news of the French attack got out at the Duchess of Richmond's ball and 'girls in flower-like dresses who had stopped laughing . . . clung with frail, unconscious hands to a scarlet sleeve, or the fur border of a pelisse', to the low-key ending of Charles Audley's romance. Bad Barbara has helped nurse the wounded, and Charles comes back without an arm: 'The vision of the conquering hero, who should have come riding gallantly back to her, faded from her mind. Reality was less romantic than her imaginings, but not less dear; and his feeble laugh and expostulation when she fed him with her grandmother's prescribed gruel were more precious to her than the most ardent love-making could have been.'

This is another scene that casts a light on Georgette Heyer's attitude to romance. She was unromantic as Jane Austen was, or Dr Johnson. 'Clear your mind of cant,' could have been her motto. She loathed pretentiousness, and hypocrisy, and self-deception. There is a touching little scene in *An Infamous Army* where Peregrine has been savagely dressed down by Audley for his flirtation with Lady Barbara and returns, shamefaced, to the wife he has neglected. She understands it all: their relationship has totally changed, but he must not know:

His abasement made her uncomfortable; even though she knew it to be make believe he must be set on his pedestal again. She said:

'Yes, we'll go home. But how shall we settle our affairs here? Will it not take some time?'

He raised his head. 'No, I'll see to everything . . . Don't worry: I'll do it all.'

He was climbing back on to the pedestal; they would not speak of this incident again; they would pretend, each one of them, that it had not happened. In the end, Peregrine would believe that it had not, and Harriet would pretend, even to herself, because there were some truths it was better not to face.

It may be a touching scene, but it is not Georgette Heyer's recipe for a good marriage: Audley and Barbara will do better, on their hard-come-by basis of realism. In the best of her books, the happy ending is genuine because the hero and heroine have fought their way to an understanding in the course of the story. It is no wonder if she was infuriated by fans who thought her books all moonlight and roses, who called them 'sweetly pretty' and consumed them avidly along with boxes of soft-centred chocolates.

Royal Escape was an attempt at what would be called faction today, a fictionalized description of Charles II's escape after the Battle of Worcester, and Georgette Heyer researched it as thoroughly as usual. The young woman who typed up *An Infamous Army* from Georgette Heyer's dictation of her handwritten script remembers visiting her a year later and spending happy days driving with her to all the Sussex inns connected with Charles's flight. The Rougiers themselves researched the remoter scene. And her notes on her reading, from the London Library, since she had found the War Office Library unsympathetic, show her meticulous as always, with the various different texts for Charles's escape set out in parallel, annotated columns.

As in *An Infamous Army*, it is possible to see just where she breathes her own life into the careful record, as in a sudden outbreak of lively dialogue between John Day and Colonel Gunter towards the end of the book: 'Master, master, you'll go from little good to stark naught . . .' or, 'Dull as a beetle, and looks besides like one which has eaten his bedstraw.' But in the main she was inhibited by the very richness of her sources. She puts a ripple of amusement into the King's voice from time to time, but cannot bring him to life. Partly because of the limitations imposed by the plot, there is a failure of tension in Charles's relationship with the people around him. This is a book in the male-centred tradition of *The Great Roxhythe* and *The Conqueror* and shares their weaknesses. And, for once, deep herself in the complicated facts of Charles's escape, Georgette Heyer fails to make its details clear to the reader. The book sold fewer copies than *The Talisman Ring* or *An Infamous Army*, but not significantly so. She was very much mistress of her public by now.

(Left) *Juana Maria Smith. From a picture painted in Paris in 1815. Harry Smith's Spanish bride was then seventeen and had been married three years since their lightning courtship after the capture of Badajoz.*
(Right) *Harry Smith, later Lieut. General Sir Harry Smith. Georgette Heyer based* The Spanish Bride *on his autobiography, written, he said, 'at full gallop'.*

She only published one title, *No Wind of Blame*, a Hemingway detective story, in 1939. Their life was changing drastically. Ronald achieved his lifetime ambition and was called to the Bar that year. If he was to succeed, he needed to be in closer touch with London, but war was imminent and Richard only seven. They compromised by moving first briefly to a flat in Steyning Mansions, Brighton, and then to a service flat at 25 Adelaide Crescent, Hove, where a short walk to Hove station put Ronald in easy commuting distance from London. Old enough not to be affected by conscription when war did break out, he served in the Home Guard and made the most of his chances at the Bar, while his wife fire-watched intrepidly. He was later to say that she never showed fear, maintaining an icy calm equally in face of a

47

charging rhinoceros or a war-time bomb. It was a characteristic shared by many of her heroines.

The owner's wife at Adelaide Crescent became a good friend and remembers Georgette Heyer as the easiest of tenants, immensely well informed and somebody everyone loved. Relieved of domestic and rationing responsibility, since the flats had no cooking facilities and all meals were provided, she used to sit by the fire, writing *The Spanish Bride* on her knee, while Richard ran wild with the owners' daughter in the gardens of the crescent, to which the tenants had keys. The result of this liberation was the publication of two books in 1940, *The Spanish Bride* and *The Corinthian*.

Georgette Heyer had discovered the *Autobiography of Sir Harry Smith* when she was doing the research for *An Infamous Army*, the only one of her books in which she allowed herself a brief bibliography. And she had undoubtedly fallen in love with Brigade-Major Smith's Spanish wife, Juana, the heroine of *The Spanish Bride*. Harry Smith's *Autobiography* was a goldmine as both a military and a personal source, but she also worked her way carefully through Cope's *History of the Rifle Brigade*, annotating it with extracts from Harry Smith, in red ink, John Kincaid's *Adventures of the Rifle Brigade* in purple and other sources individually identified in blue.

This time she brought her material brilliantly to life, achieving an unusual and satisfactory balance between the male and female interest. The relationship between fourteen-year-old Juana and the man she accepted the day she met him might have been designed for her. It is a highly unromantic romance, with Harry and Juana fighting their way to an understanding, but on this one occasion the physical side of marriage is allowed to play its part, from the wedding night through the realism of: 'She never denied the comfort of her body to Harry, though he came to her grimed with dust,' and a splendid public row on a dance floor (to be used again in *Sylvester*), to the final summary of happy marriage: 'The quiet house seemed to be full of his energetic personality; his voice shouting to her for God's sake to come at once, because he could not find his neckcloth, was the sweetest music she had heard for months.'

But Juana's story is really subsidiary to that of the Peninsular campaign, which is told with all the grasp and vividness Georgette Heyer had shown in her description of Waterloo. She can understand and describe not only the day-to-day marches and counter-marches of army and enemy but also Wellington's overall strategy, and, best of all, she can keep the reader spell-bound by that description. Deep in her subject, she throws up an occasional brilliant portrait sketch. Wellington: 'The fact was that his lordship, whose censure was masterly, had never learnt how to praise.' Or the Prince Regent meeting Harry: 'His debts, his matrimonial affairs, his quarrels with his daughter, the vulgarity of his expensive tastes, his succession of mistresses, were all perfectly well known even to a young officer from the Peninsula.' But in a few moments he has Harry 'perfectly at his ease, securely mounted on his own hobby-horse. He was astonished at the grasp of military affairs shown by the Regent.' This is Prince Florizel to the life.

The Corinthian shows Georgette Heyer back in her private world. Its hero, Beau Wyndham, is a classic case of what she described as her hero, Mark II: 'Suave, well-dressed, rich, and a famous whip,' as opposed to Mark I: 'The brusque, savage sort with a foul temper.' She had tried her hand at this deceptively elegant young man with iron beneath the silk in earlier books, but this is the first time he gets a full description:

He was a very notable Corinthian. From his Windswept hair (most difficult of all styles to achieve), to the toes of his gleaming Hessians, he might have posed as an advertisement for the Man of Fashion. His fine shoulders set off a coat of superfine cloth to perfection, his cravat, which had excited George's admiration, had been arranged by the hands of a master; his waistcoat was chosen with a nice eye; his biscuit-coloured pantaloons showed not one crease; and his Hessians with their jaunty gold tassels, had not only been made for him by Hoby, but were polished, George suspected, with a blacking mixed with champagne. A quizzing-glass on a black ribbon hung round his neck; a fob at his waist; and in one hand he carried a Sèvres snuff-box. His air proclaimed his unutterable boredom, but no tailoring, no amount of studied nonchalance, could conceal the muscle in his thighs, or the strength of his shoulders. Above the starched points of his shirt-collar, a weary, handsome face showed its owner's disillusionment. Heavy lids drooped over grey eyes which were intelligent enough, but only to observe the vanities of the world; the smile which just touched that resolute mouth seemed to mock the follies of Sir Richard's fellow men.

Naturally, when adventure comes his way in the shape of the heroine, in boy's clothes, climbing out of her bedroom window, Wyndham abandons the pose of unutterable boredom and greets it with open, if inebriate, arms. This is the last of the novels in which the hero falls in love with the heroine in male disguise. Georgette Heyer may have felt that she had taken the implications of the masquerade far enough. On the other hand *The Corinthian* resembles *Regency Buck* and *The Talisman Ring* in its thriller elements, and has one of her rare deaths. Even in the detective stories, she dealt out murder with a sparing hand. There is a murder in *The Reluctant Widow* and one in *The Toll-Gate*, but after that not even a death until that odd book, *Cousin Kate*. It is no wonder her readers feel safe with Georgette Heyer. Hers is a world where manners and morals will always triumph in the end, and without bloodshed either.

Doubleday, who had published *Death in the Stocks* as *Merely Murder* in New York, called *The Corinthian, Beau Wyndham*. It has many of the elements that were to give their characteristic charm to the Georgette Heyers, with a particularly delightful relationship between the hero, who falls in love at first sight, and the heroine, who looks on him as a benevolent uncle, imagining herself still in love with her priggish childhood sweetheart, another of Georgette Heyer's inimitable male prudes. And a minor character, Cedric Brandon, develops in the course of the book into one of her favourite characters, the light-hearted young man about town. Another new character is Lady Luttrell, the intelligent, strong-minded older woman, a pleasant change from Georgette Heyer's gallery of female grumblers. She was well endowed with aunts on both sides of the family, so there is no need to credit her knowledge of the vagaries of the older woman entirely to her widowed mother.

Life was expensive in those early years of the war, and barristers do not begin to earn at once. While she was writing the most light-hearted and entertaining of her books, Georgette Heyer was coping with all kinds of external pressures. Like all well brought up English boys of the era, Richard was despatched to prep school at the early age of eight, in 1940, and even in those days, private schooling was not cheap. Both the Heyer brothers were in the armed forces, and therefore provided for, but just the same Georgette was reduced to selling three of her back titles outright to Heinemann in 1940. They were *These Old Shades*, *Devil's Cub* and *Regency Buck*, and Heinemann paid her £750 for the British and Commonwealth rights in all three. That was a good deal of money in those days, but they got a bargain just the same. Her friend A. S. Frere later offered her the rights back for the sum she had received for them, but always the gentleman, as he described her, she said her word was her bond, and refused the offer.

Faro's Daughter, published in 1941, combines elements of the early romantic adventure stories with some admirable comedy. It has a fine example of a Mark I hero, descended from Mr Rochester by way of Devil Andover. Tall and dark, Ravenscar has 'a lean, harsh-featured countenance with an uncompromising mouth and extremely hard grey eyes'. He falls into instant dislike for the Amazonian heroine, Deb Grantham, who helps her aunt run a gaming house, and they spar like Beatrice and Benedick throughout the book. Georgette Heyer did not let herself quote Shakespeare much, but her comedy owes his a great deal. She once said, 'my plots are abysmal, and I think of

Evening dress, 1805.

them with blood and tears,' but this is an instance of the self-deprecatory line that grew on her through the years of critical neglect. Her family confirm that she did indeed work at her plots with blood and tears, playing innumerable games of patience, plunged in black gloom when things went badly, prowling restlessly about the house until she had her plan worked out, when she would sit down and write under immense pressure and at high speed, often late into the night. Like many remarkable people, she needed comparatively little sleep, and her son remembers her as writing into the small hours and thus being able to lead the normal life of wife and mother in the daytime.

Faro's Daughter has one of her most elegantly worked out plots, with surprise piled on surprise at the end. Having read it once, at speed, the connoisseur will re-read it more slowly and enjoy noticing the delicate stages by which Deb and Ravenscar fall into love. He 'began reluctantly to feel interested in the working of Miss Grantham's mind', while Deb's increasing rage with him is equally suggestive. As always in Georgette Heyer's happiest relationships, there is the bond of laughter between them. Deb has Ravenscar kidnapped, but is appalled to discover the means her accomplices have used:

'I thought they could do it without using any horrid stratagems! *That* was fair enough! There could be no possible objection, for how could I kidnap you myself?'

Mr Ravenscar was sitting in a position of considerable discomfort, with cords cutting into his wrists and ankles; and his head was aching as well, but his lips twitched at this, and he burst out laughing.

'Oh, no objection at all, Miss Grantham!'

And when her priggish brother releases him, he refuses to go, staying to fight it out with Deb through a brilliantly contrived series of misunderstandings. This is one of Georgette Heyer's funniest books and shows her unusually free with the conventions of the world she was making for herself. In none of the later books could the heroine have presided over a gaming table and still survived socially, but then this one is set in the mid-1790s, some twenty years before the Regency period she was to make her own, and the social code was much less rigid. This was still the age when the plebeian Miss Gunnings could become duchesses.

Outside the private world, things were not going well for

Georgette Heyer at this time. Her relations with her agents, Christy & Moore, were showing signs of strain. L. P. Moore had been against the outright sale of the three titles to Heinemann, predicting tax problems, in which, in fact, he proved to be right. And her relationship with her other publisher, Hodder & Stoughton, was less happy than that with Heinemann. She had failed to achieve with that patriarchal house the personal relationship she needed with her publisher, and had found with A. S. Frere. There were various causes of friction. Paper was rationed during the war and she did not see why Hodder could not find more for her books and was furious when a director told her they could have sold six times as many copies of *No Wind of Blame* if they could only have printed them. Her friend Carola Oman was also published by Hodder, and they compared some gloomy notes. In the end, she returned in a rage from an unlucky lunch at the Ritz, having detected a fatal note of patronage in her host's tone, and vowed to leave Hodder. Her contract gave them an option on her next detective story, so she sat down and began *Penhallow*: 'Jimmy the Bastard was polishing the shoes . . .' Intended as a contract-breaking book, it was duly turned down by Hodder and published by Heinemann. Unfortunately it also ended her association with Doubleday in the United States. It was the last book of hers they published, and the last detective story she wrote for nine years.

But it was actually written with more passionate commitment than usual. Once she had thought of it, she became absorbed and had to set aside *Faro's Daughter* for a while, and rough out its characters. It is a strange, grim book, one of her few ventures into the field of tragedy, and shows more signs of strain than can be accounted for by war and trouble with agents or publishers. This was a bad time in Georgette Heyer's life, the nearest she ever came to a breakdown. A photograph taken a few years later in 1944 shows her not so much thin as gaunt, and the surface comedy of *Penhallow* is set against a dark background. An unusual prefatory quotation from *Measure for Measure* suggests that she took her subject seriously. Set in a Cornish mansion that has a touch of Cold Comfort Farm about it, this is the story of a tyrannical old grandfather, Penhallow of Trevellin, who makes his large family, including Jimmy the Bastard, live wretchedly at home under his thumb. The slow build-up to his murder has some good comic scenes as well as frank melodrama, and the book is not really a detective story at all, since the reader knows all along who the murderer is, and she escapes discovery, left only to bear the burden of guilt. There is a glum, almost at times sick atmosphere in this book that it shares with *Barren Corn* and *Cousin Kate*. Every life has its bad times, and *Penhallow* may reflect trouble in Georgette Heyer's. There were certainly changes on the way.

Chapter 3

By February 1942 the Rougiers were beginning to think of moving to London. It had been a bad winter. Ronald's widowed mother had died after a distressing illness just after Christmas, and Georgette Heyer herself had not been well and had finally caught whooping cough from Richard. 'Life has not been either very easy or very pleasant during the past three months,' she wrote a cousin of Ronald's who was overseas with the army, and went on to apologize for her writing paper: 'There's a shortage of paper for authors and publishers – though not, believe me, for disgusting doyleys, pie-collars, and all other such useless fripperies, and certainly not for any Government department.' She was always a passionate hater of bureaucrats.

Ronald was increasingly busy at the Bar and was finding the daily train journey exhausting in those days of blitz and blacked-out stations and uncertain trains, and Georgette Heyer was missing her friends. They seized a chance that year to fulfil a long ambition of hers and rent chambers in Albany where her publisher friend A. S. Frere lived. Albany House, once the home of the first Lord Melbourne and then of George II's son, the Duke of York and Albany, had been turned into bachelor chambers by the early nineteenth century and had been occupied by such famous figures as 'Monk' Lewis, Lord Byron and Lord Macaulay, who described it as a college life in the centre of London. It is indeed a remarkably protected oasis of quiet off Piccadilly just west of Piccadilly Circus, and for

Albany, by Dennis Flanders. The Rougiers' home for 24 years. Georgette Heyer fulfilled a long ambition by moving there in 1942.

Georgette Heyer it had another advantage; it was close to the London Library. She did not like working in libraries, but could comfortably carry off her town member's ration of ten books at a time. Their chambers, F3 Albany, were reached by a gruelling flight of concrete steps, but were spacious when you got there, with the handsome sitting room and study Georgette Heyer always wanted, a kitchen tucked away up a spiral staircase, and two attic spare bedrooms, in theory for servants, but one of which was in fact used as a base by Boris Heyer. Richard was at school, but home for the holidays with a special dispensation of the Albany rule against children. The family also included his mother's white bull terrier, Johnny. 'It's only the man with the white dog,' said Jermyn Street prostitutes when Ronald walked him last thing at night. There was supposed to be a friendly haunt by Lord Macaulay, but only Johnny noticed this much. Georgette Heyer made a good story of the haunt, but always mocked the supernatural in her books.

And the bad time, whatever it had been, was passing. Georgette Heyer published no book in 1943, the first blank year since 1927, but that November she wrote cheerfully to Louisa Callender, A. S. Frere's assistant at Heinemann, to describe the book she was working on:

> It is a Regency society-comedy quite in my lightest vein. There is a certain young man who has appeared in several of my books – he was Cedric Brandon in *The Corinthian*, Viscount Winwood in *The Convenient Marriage* – and some others! And once I said idly that I would one day write a frivolous story about that young man. This is it. This time he is Viscount Sheringham (Sherry), the story begins with his runaway marriage to a very young lady whom he's known since childhood, and with whom he isn't in the least in love. And the story is about all the circumstances which lead (a) to his partial reform and (b) to his falling in love with his wife (of course!) . . . Nothing mysterious or very exciting happens, but I think it is pretty lively. The title is *Friday's Child* . . . I've done about 55,000 words, so I should think another three weeks ought to see it finished, but I won't promise.

Since *Friday's Child* is well over 100,000 words, this gives some idea of the speed at which Georgette Heyer habitually wrote. When she was writing, she preferred to do nothing else. Her daughter-in-law, later, would know she had started a book when her daily telephone calls ceased, and she herself once summed it up: 'I'm not dining out till I've finished *Duplicate Death.*'

Twenty years later, Georgette Heyer described *Friday's Child* as 'my own favourite', and it shows her writing at her apparently effortless, entertaining best. It is one of her books best not read in public places, such as trains, for fear of being disgraced by fits of uncontrollable laughter. It has, as she said herself, 'Some very peerless characters, including George, Lord Wrotham, who . . . is for ever trying to fight duels with his friends; and Mr Ringwood and the Hon. Ferdy Fakenham, who are quite dumb, but very good value.' They are indeed, but there is more to the book than its comedy. The perceptive reader is well aware that the girl Sherry marries for a whim has always loved him, and when she is finally driven to run away from him, the book is close to being what Lady Caroline Lamb called a 'crying' one. Laughing at her own work, Georgette Heyer never laughed at this aspect of it, and it is the one that her imitators have found inimitable.

While she wrote it, she was being plagued by the first of many battles with the Inspector of Taxes. This one went back to the outright sale of three back titles to Heinemann in 1940. She had claimed that this was a capital sum and therefore untaxable; the Inspector regarded it as income, and taxable. By 1944, the Inspector of Taxes had taken the question to appeal, and won. Ronald Rougier argued the case himself instead of getting in a tax expert, and never forgot his defeat, which left them both convinced that the tax man was their enemy. The strain of this battle may show in that gaunt photograph of 1944.

Friday's Child came out that year, was taken by Putnam in New York, and had a printing of over 110,000 in England, and a Foyles Book Club edition of 172,500, but the tax burden continued heavy, Albany was expensive and Richard now at public school. Georgette Heyer was not too proud at this time to read and report on books for her friend Frere, for the small fee publishers pay for this privilege. Heinemann were paying about two guineas at this time. Georgette Heyer obviously enjoyed the reading and did it well, with a good eye, Frere remembers, for the marketable. One of her letter reports survives, and is worth quoting:

> Sorry: I've taken an unpardonably long time over *In Me My Enemy*. What with Frank's leave, and Richard going to Marlborough, and myself having flu, I've had no time to think of books.
>   Well, you can't handle it. It's all very difficult, but I do seem to be sure about that. I think she has got something. She can tell a story, she has a gift of phrase, and the fact that she can't spell or punctuate doesn't really matter. What does matter is that here is a huge, inchoate mass of a book, without rhyme or reason, over-weighted, and degenerating, in its last third, into melodrama.

After a long and acute analysis of the book, she concludes:

> 'Don't be too ambitious!' is impossible advice to give to a young author, but it is the right advice here. The girl has the makings of a romantic novelist, not of a great, gloomy, introspective saga-writer. I should advise her to put this book in a drawer; to think out a good, close-knit plot with plenty of wild deeds and dark passions, and a nice, fat climax; to limit herself to 100,000 words; not to stray into the bogs of psychology – and to get on with it! She would write a seller if she would limit her horizons and see her book as a whole before she sets pen to paper.

After this report, which is everything a publisher's heart could desire, Georgette Heyer goes on to remark, in passing, that she has 'a book going round in my own head like a borer beetle', and ends, 'How much sordid cash am I getting out of the old firm this autumn? Can I afford a new fur coat?' The report would hardly have paid for one, but the book in her head must have been *The Reluctant Widow*, which was published, after another of the rare blank years, in 1946. Georgette Heyer's own favourite photograph, taken that year, shows her at her elegant best, the bad time obviously over. *The Reluctant Widow* is dedicated to Richard, who was now fourteen and well able to enjoy its combination of romantic comedy and thriller plot. After her death, Ronald Rougier insisted that his wife never drew any of her characters from life, but it is hard not to see Richard's influence in the engaging series of very young men and boys in *The Reluctant Widow*, *The Foundling*, *Arabella* and *The Grand Sophy*, all written while he was in his teens. The Mark II hero of *The Reluctant Widow* has an engaging young brother Nicholas, rusticated from his university because of an irresistible bear. The book also has the first of such delightful dogs as the mongrel in *Arabella* and the 'Baluchistan hound' in *Frederica*. Georgette Heyer may have mocked her fans, but she knew how to engage their interest. Despite its two violent deaths, *The Reluctant Widow* is one of her most light-hearted books, with some unusually broad comedy and a delicious merry war between its common-sense heroine and the hero whom she describes as 'the most odious, overbearing, inconsiderate, abominable man I ever met'. To which his sister replies: 'Famous! How often I have said the same! You will deal admirably together.'

1947 was another blank year. Georgette Heyer was writing *The Foundling* and not altogether happy about it. '*I* think it lacks sparkle. Perhaps I'm growing old. Ronald wants me to jack up the Regency and do a Worth-While book again. Says also that it was the Army that put me on the map, and why not start a big book.' But serial rights in *The Foundling* had been bought by *Woman's Journal* for £1,000 on the strength of the first third of the book, 'which stinks', said Georgette Heyer, who had a curious hate-love relationship with Miss Sutherland, editor of *Woman's Journal*. She had been affronted when Miss Sutherland turned down *Friday's Child* for serialization, and 'was kind enough to write and tell me what was wrong with the book'. Now she said that she 'always likes my worst work'. Miss Sutherland, reciprocating the hate-love, nevertheless recognized that when she ran one of Georgette Heyer's books as a serial every copy of *Woman's Journal* sold out,

With her son Richard in his teens. Public schooling was not cheap.

and remembers that men snatched the new issue from their wives' hands in order to read the latest instalment.

The Foundling appeared in 1948 and most certainly does not lack sparkle. It has another delightful boy, constantly in trouble, and the foundling herself is one of Georgette Heyer's marvellously silly young women, ready to go off with anyone who offers her a silk dress, preferably purple. And the plausible villain, Liversedge, who kidnaps the hero and then makes himself indispensable to him, is an admirable comic creation. The book is to a remarkable extent a boys' adventure story, but has a touching, if lightly etched in, relationship between hero and heroine, reluctantly engaged at the beginning of the book and happily to be married at the end. Of course, Harriet, like Kitten in *Friday's Child*, has been in love all the time. In the Heyer world

Beau Brummell, the famous dandy and friend of the Prince Regent. He fled the country (and his debts) in 1816, so appears only in the books set earlier.

heroes are always freer agents than heroines, which does not make it entirely unlike the real one.

The publicity manager at Heinemann tried to persuade Georgette Heyer to allow some personal detail in the promotion of *The Foundling*, but wrote resignedly: 'Well, there shall be no letters to the Press about Mrs Rougier — "The Regency character who lives in the very Quarters of the old Bucks". Nor any paragraphs about her mythical country place in Sussex. Nor any picture (with or without ear-rings).' He ended that there were 'two people who want to interview you. But I see no reason why you should not stick to your decision to cut this out.' Georgette Heyer never saw any reason to change her stand about this. When Frere himself made some mild proposal about a publicity

Mr Jackson giving instruction at his rooms in Bond Street, by Cruikshank.
Most heroes had iron muscles under their well-tailored coats, but Freddy, in
Cotillion, *did not aspire to 'pop in a hit under Jackson's guard'.*

lunch at the Savoy in the Thirties she threatened to appear with
her enormous wolfhound bitch. 'Or shall I just come as Little Me
– really the *simplest* of creatures, happiest when pottering about
my kitchen?' He never repeated the suggestion.

The move to London marked a critical stage so far as
Georgette Heyer's passion for privacy was concerned. That was
the moment when she could conveniently have started giving
interviews; have made public appearances, joined clubs and
become a public person. And she had decided most definitely
against it. With a few exceptions, she did not think very highly of
her fellow authors, whom she tended to dismiss as 'inkies', and
she did not even join the Society of Authors, which had not
helped her over the tax case of 1944, presumably because she
was not a member. She described her stand about publicity in a
letter of 1955, and it never changed: 'As for being photographed
At Work or In My Old World Garden, that is the type of
publicity which I find nauseating and quite unnecessary. My
private life concerns no one but myself and my family; and if, on
the printed page, I am Miss Heyer, everywhere else I am Mrs

Rougier, who makes no public appearances and dislikes few things so much as being confronted by Fans. There seems to be a pathetic belief today in the power of personal publicity over sales. I don't share it . . .

'Console yourself with the thought that my answers to the sort of questions Fans ask seem to daunt them a bit! Not unnaturally, they expect me to be a Romantic, and I'm nothing of the sort.'

What must have maddened her was the way fans and critics, concentrating on the romance, ignored the style of her books, and the hard, detailed work that went into them. It would have been nearer the mark if she had said that she was not *only* a romantic. By now, she was so deeply grounded in the late eighteenth and early nineteenth centuries that she could date a book effortlessly by the most casual of references to contemporary events. She hardly ever uses an actual flat-footed date. In *The Foundling*, for instance, an early reference to the Prince Regent sets the book after 1811, one to Waterloo then tells us it is after 1815, and one to Princess Charlotte's death in childbirth finally places it after 1817. It is almost a game that she plays with the reader, and one who joins her in it will not catch her in error. Similarly, her background detail is impeccable. If she remarks that 'the sum of one pound was paid to the Post Office every year . . . to ensure the early delivery of the mail,' it is because she knows this. When she refers, again in *The Foundling*, to Mr Liversedge's blackmailer's bible, Thomas Goddard's *Biographical Index to the Present House of Lords*, one knows the book was in her invaluable reference library, which amounted to some thousand books by the time of her death. A. S. Byatt saw and described this library: 'The OED, the DNB, Lemprière, dictionaries of slang, dialect, Anglo Saxon, Fowler, Roget, Debrett, Burke, an 1808 dictionary to the House of Lords [Mr Liversedge's bible], proverbs, place-names, foreign phrases . . . standard historical works in both the mediaeval and the eighteenth-century periods . . . histories of snuff-boxes, of sign-posts, and coaching . . . several shelves on costume from Planché's two-volume *Cyclopedia of Costume* (1876) to Alison Adburgham on *Shops and Shopping*,

Grand-Cartaret's *Les Elégances de la Toilette* to *The History of Underclothes*.'

With all this research material at hand, and scrupulously consulted, it is no wonder if she disliked the fans and critics who wrote of her as if she were just another purveyor of romantic candy floss. Fans who wrote and asked sensible historical questions got answered and so did the ones who asked about her language. Late in her life her then publisher, The Bodley Head, had a serious enquiry from a Canadian, about the phrase 'Cheltenham tragedy', which appears for the first time in *The Foundling*. He had been unable to find the phrase in any dictionary, he said, and had discussed its provenance with a group of American academics, one of whom suggested that it referred to Mrs Siddons's early provincial success in Cheltenham. Georgette Heyer must have been delighted with this respectful letter, but she had to say that she could not remember where she found the phrase, though she knew she had not made it up. Her two files of vocabulary do not give their sources: she was a collector, not a scholar. In fact, the Cheltenham phrase does not show up under 'Trouble', though one finds *hubble-bubble*, a *Scarborough warning*, and to *come home by Weeping Cross*; or under 'Talk', which has *roundaboutation, scandal-broth* and *pishery pashery*. She must have used it direct from something she was reading.

Perhaps it was in a mood of irritation with critics and fans alike that Georgette Heyer wrote early in 1948 that she had, 'yielded to the persuasions (some might call it nagging) of Husband and Publisher, and am now committed to what Frere calls a Real Book. That is, if I ever recover from the profound inertia which at present envelops me.' She and her husband had been on holiday in Ireland at Christmas and, she said, 'I have never been the same woman since.' She never could like the Irish. Obviously Ronald and, it seems, Frere had continued to urge the worthwhile book like *An Infamous Army*, which, according to Ronald, had put her on the map. In fact, *An Infamous Army* had sold less well than *The Spanish Bride*, and significantly less well than *These Old Shades, Devil's Cub, Friday's Child,* or *The Reluctant Widow.* But it was not the financial map they were talking about. Georgette Heyer had been an established best-seller for years, and not only in England. When Frere went to Australia just after the war, it was her books that were demanded by booksellers, and he went straight home and found extra paper for them. The Australians had always been fond of her, and a librarian wrote describing her as a 'bonzer woman' and reporting that: 'All the girls who read the filthiest books like yours.'

She had not achieved anything like the same success in the United States, where she had been without a publisher between 1931 and 1935 and again between 1943 and 1946, when Putnam published *Friday's Child* two years after its English publication. She said herself that she was only selling seven or eight thousand copies in the United States at this time. But she was being steadily and profitably serialized in England, and *The Reluctant Widow* was being filmed. She could afford to consider status as well as earnings. She had immensely enjoyed the research for *The Conqueror, An Infamous Army, Royal Escape* and *The Spanish Bride,* and the last three had been treated with respect. There is always an element of patronage in any praise romantic novels get, and if there was one thing Georgette Heyer could not bear it was to be patronized. She would go back to that early love of hers and write an historical biography, the kind of book that got her friend Carola Oman such respectful reviews.

She chose as her subject Henry V's younger brother, John, Duke of Bedford, an attractive man and able administrator, who outlived his brother and became guardian and right-hand man to his unlucky nephew, Henry VI. It was a bold project indeed, but she had a nucleus of early notes already, those for *Simon the Coldheart,* and knew where to start. Now she began to collect information, fact by fact, about people and events in Great Britain and France for the years of John's life, 1389 to 1435. Three card indexes cover this period, itemized by year, month and day. The first one has just one entry, on its own card: *1389, 20th June, Birth of John.* The last four entries are all for December

1431 when John's nephew, Henry VI, entered Paris in triumph and was crowned there. The cards show that in the course of that year Joan of Arc, who had been captured the year before, had been tried and finally executed. Blank cards dated to 1435 should have covered the rest of John's career up to his death in September 1435, but they were never filled in. The project had proved too vast.

For the moment, it was a fascinating pursuit, and one after Georgette Heyer's heart. A file of modern words and phrases translated into mediaeval English records that languor is *wanlust*, quarrelsome is *branglesome* or *frampold*, and a sweetheart an *amourette*, and, added in pencil to the original typed column, a sweetmeat a *dariote, dragé* or *doucet*. A biographical file begins with Anne of Bohemia, 'Far too meek and under R's thumb' (R being her husband, Richard II), and ends with two neatly written pages on Edward, Duke of York. This is complemented by a card index of biographies, running from the dukes of Alençon to Richard, Duke of York, who 'did not marry Cecily Neville till after 1435'. A file of mediaeval phrases is strong on 'Church', and 'Hawking' and 'Horses', gives twenty-four words for fools, from *dodipoll* unalphabetically to *beetlehead* and is full of useful information about, for instance, the canonical hours, from matins – before daybreak – through tierce at nine, to compline, bedtime.

Other files cover: Castles and Abbeys; Arms and Armour; Heraldry and Sport, Household; Manners; State Officers and Papacy; Topography; Chronicles, Memoirs and Miscellaneous; and Social. They are thick with information of every kind, the treasured collection of many years, and perhaps inevitably somewhat random in their organization. Their collector would doubtless have known that the Hanseatic League and Hoccleve would both be found under Social, whereas Froissart comes under Chronicles, Memoirs and Miscellaneous. It is not surprising that Georgette Heyer always found it a struggle to get back into this project.

She illustrated her material with maps and family trees,

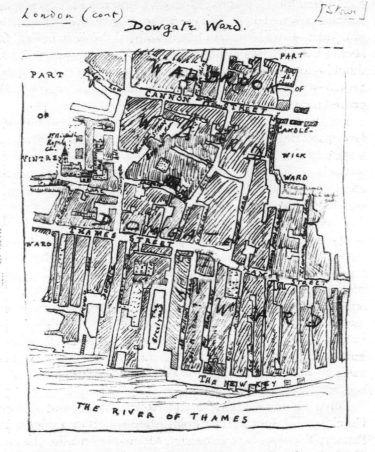

A map of Dowgate in London from Georgette Heyer's mediaeval notebooks. She had not been able to find out exactly where Cold Harbour, the Lancasters' London home, was situated

complete with carefully drawn and coloured heraldic devices and including a map of mediaeval Paris and an immensely complicated English royal family tree showing the houses of York and Lancaster before the Wars of the Roses. It was a labour of love that must have taken an immense amount of time and patience over the years. In September 1951 she wrote that she was just back from two weeks in the north with Ronald: 'A pious pilgrimage, in aid of my mediaeval book. I put no fewer than 12 ancient castles in the bag!' And there they are, complete with postcards and descriptions, in the thick file labelled Castles and Abbeys. But it must have gradually become obvious that this was a very long-term project indeed.

Georgette Heyer wrote Frere in 1949 that '*Fettered Eagle* is going to be grand.' It would have been a good title for the story of Henry V's brother, but her husband, consenting to the publication of her unfinished manuscript after her death, gave it the simpler name of *My Lord John*. He explained his decision to publish in a moving foreword:

> The fame of my wife, Georgette Heyer, rests largely upon her historical novels, particularly those of the Regency period. But this was not her favourite: she preferred what she called 'armour', the Middle Ages. She was especially attracted to that period of English history when the House of Lancaster was at its peak, from about 1393 to 1435.
>
> Some years ago she planned a work, a trilogy,[1] to illustrate this period, taking John, Duke of Bedford, the younger and most trusted brother of Henry V, as its central character, for his life-span covered the whole period, and because he was a great man though not today a well-known character. With his death the decay of the Lancastrian line set in.

And, after describing his wife's enormous and meticulous research, he went on:

> For the work, as she planned it, she needed a period of about five years' single-minded concentration. But this was not granted to her. The penal burden of British taxation, coupled

1 In fact, Georgette Heyer's letters show that she planned it for one-volume publication.

with the clamour of her readers for a new book, made her break off to write another Regency story. After such a break it was hard to recapture the spirit of her main work and a good deal of labour to refresh her knowledge. After this had happened a second time, she laid her manuscript aside, foreseeing that at least two more such interruptions would inevitably recur before she could complete the work. So a great historical novel was never finished.

Georgette Heyer's table of contents for the whole project survives. It is divided into two parts, each consisting of three sections. The first, entitled *John of Lancaster*, was to consist of:

Book I Richard the Redeless (1394–1399)
Book II The Unquiet Time (1399–1405)
Book III Prince Excellent (1410–1413)

The second part, to be titled possibly *My Lord of Bedford*, or *Right Mighty Prince*, was also to contain three books:

Book I Stark Harry (1413–1422)
Book II My Lord the Regent (1422–?)
Book III *A Vous Entière*

On this basis, the work published as *My Lord John* is in fact the first half of the planned whole, not quite finished, since Georgette Heyer left off in mid-sentence shortly before the death of Henry IV in 1413. Did she break off at this point because she realized that, though she had covered twenty of her planned forty years, she was far from being half way through in terms of content, with the eventful reign of Henry V and the disastrous one of Henry VI all to come? For her book to be the great historical novel her mourning husband claimed, it would have needed heavy cutting in this first surviving section.

It would have needed more than that. Georgette Heyer had a romantic passion for the Middle Ages and most particularly for

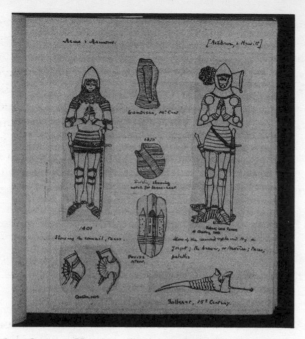

A page from Georgette Heyer's mediaeval notebooks. Her husband said she liked to refer to the Middle Ages as 'armour'.

the House of Lancaster who, she said, on meeting the last member of the family at a party, always had such good manners. But this was perhaps the one time in her life when her lack of formal education handicapped her. Her cool, rational intelligence was instinctively at home in the mental climate of the late eighteenth and early nineteenth centuries, and what she did not understand by instinct could easily be researched in the wealth of contemporary material available to her. But the Middle Ages were a different matter. Those were the days when religion dominated men's lives: heaven and hell were real places; the flat earth was the centre of the universe, and one might always hope to hear the music of the spheres. Georgette Heyer could not make her characters think like mediaeval people and, fatally, she could not make them talk like them either. Here, too, the difference between modern and eighteenth-century English is minimal compared with that between modern and mediaeval. Anyone can understand a page of Jane Austen; it takes practice to read Chaucer or Langland. Their language is deeply grounded in Anglo-Saxon, Norman-French and Church Latin and it defeated Georgette Heyer. Her husband said that she became adept at reading mediaeval English, but writing it was another matter. It was not enough simply to collect words and phrases; they had to be put together. The narrative style of *My Lord John* is often stilted and the dialogue seldom quite comes off, swinging disastrously between modern slang and unconvincing mediaeval phrases:

> Well, if I was, I repented me, didn't I? If I hadn't dropped a hint in your father's ear, he would have been keycold now, and you too, I daresay! And what is my guerdon? Unthank! And in all belikelihood my head set up on the bridge for the crows to peck at!

This was the last and least successful of the books Georgette Heyer centred around the hero. It had never been her happiest vein and this time the hero, though a sterling man, was not a compelling enough central figure. She went on referring to the project with enthusiasm, but there were moments of doubt too. Putnam in New York showed great interest. In 1952 she meant to let them 'see John of Bedford before any other US publisher', but by 1955 she had changed her mind. 'I have no intention of letting them handle *John of Lancaster*,' she wrote Frere. But: 'It does seem to me that JOHN's hope lies in the States. I don't mean that you won't be able to sell it: you will, but not, I think, in huge quantities. Admirers of two recent works of unhistorical fiction – one about Katherine Swynford,[1] and the other about Catherine de Valois, Q. of England – will not at all relish my book. At the same time, I've little doubt that when American publishers say that they want books about the Middle Ages they

1 Presumably Anya Seton's *Katherine*, published the previous year.

have in mind a welter of flesh, blood, sadism, and general violence. Breast-sellers, in fact. Well, life wasn't like that under the Lancastrian kings – torture, for instance, was not employed in England until a later date: did you know that? – and my book isn't going to satisfy the seekers after Peculiar Sensations. So that I might find it difficult to place in the States . . . I've reached the halfway mark – perhaps! . . . Reading it through, I myself think it isn't at all bad . . . it may bore you stiff.'

She must have written almost all of *My Lord John* at this point, since she says, 'I haven't yet reached the death of Henry IV (Jerusalem Chamber), and, with it, the end of Part III, Prince Excellent.' She did not show it to Frere, nor did she mean to let Miss Sutherland see it. Soon afterwards she wrote: 'I never felt less like writing a gay romance, am churning out heavy pastry in a slow laborious fashion . . . When I sit and try to think about it, I find, after half an hour, that I have mentally written the whole of Henry IV's death-bed scene. Blast everything! When I once again laid John of Lancaster in lavender, I felt as I did when I saw Richard off to his Prep school for the first time.'

She never did write Henry IV's death-bed scene. The demands of the fans and the tax man always supervened. Or that is what she said. It is hard to believe, however, that the instinct that steered her through her first experimental years was not operating here too. To please the noisier fans, and pay the taxes, she should have gone on writing *These Old Shades* and *Devil's Cub* for ever. But *The Convenient Marriage* and *Regency Buck* had shown her where her genius lay. To write romantic comedy as supremely well as she did, she must have enjoyed it. Everyone who knew her confirms that she was a compulsive writer, and this is what she compulsively wrote best. She has to have known this, and all the deprecatory talk about its stinking was meant to fob off the outside world that liked the wrong things for the wrong reasons. Unfinished, her mediaeval project was at once a splendid hobby and a claim to the respectability denied to 'mere' entertainers. Finished, it might have proved a sad disappointment.

Chapter 4

Georgette Heyer first mentioned her mediaeval project to Frere in the spring of 1948, but by that autumn she had realized that it would be a long job and that she must keep producing the books that sold. In September she was considering a book about George, Lord Wrotham, the belligerent minor character from *Friday's Child*, but by October she was 'very busy with Arabella, who is a nice wench, and giving me a lot of fun. As for Mr Beaumaris, the fans will fall for him in rows, because he's their favourite hero.' As usual, she was writing fast: 'I've done about 20,000 words, so it is safe to say that the book will be in your hands before Christmas.' In fact, Frere acknowledged the 'beautifully typed' manuscript on 16 November. By now Georgette Heyer, who had originally written her books in longhand, some of them even with an eighteenth-century quill pen, had yielded to modernism and composed straight on to a heavy old-fashioned typewriter, described by an American visitor as almost a museum piece. Like its successors, it had been modified with special keys to suit her very precise requirements.

Arabella was one of the books written into the small hours, with passionate intensity and a little gin and benzedrine when necessary. Arabella herself is indeed a nice wench and comes from one of Georgette Heyer's rare happy families. The opening scenes at the Yorkshire vicarage are particularly delightful, with a classic one where mother and daughters go through her old trunks to find the materials for Arabella's London wardrobe. This shows

Georgette Heyer at her knowledgeable best, aware not only of fashion but of changes in fashion:

The stiff, voluminous silks and brocades Mama had worn, with their elaborate undergowns, and their pads, and their wired bodices seemed not only archaic, but very ugly too. What was this funny jacket, with all the whale-bone? A Caraco? Gracious! And this striped thing, for all the world like a dressing-gown? A lustring sack – well, it was certainly very like a sack, to be sure! Did Mama wear it in *company*? What was in this elegant box? *Poudre à la Maréchale*! But did Mama then powder her hair, like the picture of Grandmama Tallant, up at the Hall? Oh, *not* quite like that! A *gray* powder? Oh, Mama, no! and you without a gray hair to your head! How did you dress it? Not cut *at all*? Curls to the waist at the back? And all those rolls and puffs over the ears! How could Mama have had the patience to do it? So odd as it must have looked, too!

Arabella is the classic story of Cinderella launched into society, but its heroine has the advantage of having been the local beauty in Yorkshire: 'No fool, the little Tallant.' Having rashly described herself as an heiress in order to give the rich hero a set-down, she depresses the pretensions of one fortune-hunter after another and keeps even the eligible Mr Beaumaris at arms' length until her young brother's debts compel him to take refuge from the law in a sordid London slum. The only way she can think of to extricate him is to accept Mr Beaumaris, but she must go further; she needs money at once; they must elope. Luckily for her, Mr Beaumaris has seen through it all, and takes her not to Gretna Green but to his grandmother's house in Wimbledon, where, instead of being ravished as she fears, she is given hot milk and put to bed, alone. Georgette Heyer is beginning to enjoy turning upside down the romantic clichés she herself had helped to make popular, and the book ends in one of her longest scenes of pure comedy, culminating in Arabella's awed discovery that her elegant love has spent a happy evening discussing Wolf's

Coat of arms of John, Duke of Bedford, hero of My Lord John. *From Georgette Heyer's notebooks. She spent long, loving hours in the study copying heraldic devices for her mediaeval book.*

Prolegomena ad Homerum with her formidable father. Georgette Heyer's brother, a classicist, remembers being applied to by his sister for the title of the required learned work.

1949 was an exhausting year. 'Very much harassed at the moment by Family Upheavals,' wrote Georgette Heyer to a friend in May. 'An aged aunt has had a slight stroke . . . You get the set-up! One aunt of 84, the "stroked" one 6 years younger . . .

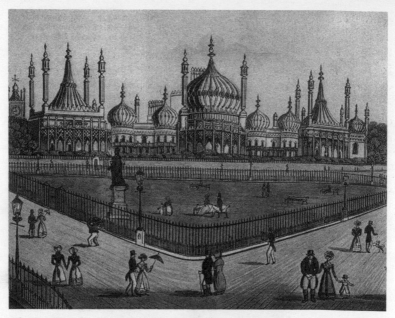

The Pavilion, the Prince Regent's country house at Brighton, which he turned into a palace. 'A captious critic had once remarked . . . that it was as though St Paul's had littered and brought forth a rash of cupolas.' Regency Buck

My mamma and I are going round in circles.' A friend said of Georgette Heyer that she never put on writer's airs, or was too busy to see her friends, and this was just as true of her family. She was entirely its centre now and had also taken a firm place in the Rougier clan. When Ronald's cousin, Dmitri Tornow, was sent overseas at the beginning of the war, he gave Georgette Heyer's name as next of kin since they were then uncertain where Ronald might be.

By the autumn of 1949, Georgette Heyer had a new cause for anxiety. *The Reluctant Widow* was being filmed and she did not at all like the way things were going: 'I am being driven frantic by the advance publicity from Denham, and am trying to think what I can do about it. I feel as though a slug had crawled over me. *I* think it is going to do me a great deal of harm, on account of the schoolgirl public. Already I'm getting letters reproaching me. They have turned the Widow into a "bad-girl" part for Jean Kent, and this week's *Illustrated* carried two pages, headed "Jean Locks Her Bedroom Door". Also seduction scenes . . . If I had wanted a reputation for salacious novels I could have got it easily enough. The whole thing is so upsetting that it is putting me right off my stroke.' When the film appeared she wisely refused to go, and seventeen-year-old Richard, who did, came out half way through, speechless with rage.

There was a characteristic postcript to this letter: 'PS: I've done about 70,000 words of *The Grand Sophy*. My brother says it is most amusing. But I have bought a large bottle of Disinfectant.' The tone of self-mockery was getting stronger. But Sophy is grand indeed. If Georgette Heyer had two kinds of heroes, Mark I and Mark II, this is equally true of her heroines. The Mark I heroine is a tall young woman with a great deal of character and somewhat mannish habits who tends to dominate the plots of the books she appears in; the Mark II one is a quiet girl, bullied by her family, partly because she cannot bear scenes. When a Mark I heroine meets a Mark I hero, as in *Faro's Daughter*, there will be fireworks. But Charles, in *The Grand Sophy*, is a Mark I who thinks he is a Mark II. It takes Sophy's outrageous behaviour to bring out the Mark I in him and achieve the happy ending. Psychoanalysts would have a great many long words for this, but the book is one of the group of Georgette Heyers that endear her to feminists. It is also outrageously funny, with a careful build-up to one of her very best climaxes, organized by Sophy, when all the characters change partners in one comic confrontation after another, so tightly woven as to be unquotable.

The book has some admirable minor characters: Augustus Fawnhope the beautiful poet, Lord Bromford the hypochondriac, and Miss Wraxton the society prude to whom Charles is engaged. Enraged by her patronizing tone, Sophy breaks a social rule by driving down St James's Street, a male preserve in those days, but apologizes afterwards. Eugenia Wraxton, on the other hand, errs more seriously by carrying tales and admitting that she is prepared to betray a confidence in a good cause. Her surface manners may be impeccable, but this is a failure of moral humanity that puts her beyond the pale.

Like *Arabella*, this book shows Georgette Heyer beginning gently to mock the rules of her own romantic game. Quarrelling with Charles, Sophy starts to cry:

'*Sophy*!' ejaculated Mr Rivenhall, visibly shaken. He took an involuntary step towards her, checked himself, and said, rather disjointedly: 'Pray do not! I did not mean – I had no intention – You know how it is with me! I say more than I mean, when – For God's sake do not cry!'

'Oh, do not stop me!' begged Sophy. 'Sir Horace says it is my *only* accomplishment.'

Mr Rivenhall glared at her. '*What*?'

'Very few persons are able to do it,' Sophy assured him. 'I discovered it by the veriest accident when I was only seven years old. Sir Horace said I should cultivate it, for I should find it most useful.'

By now, the rules of Georgette Heyer's private world, its habits and language, were so well established as to lay her open to imitation as well as to adulation. I must plead guilty, among others. My own early books show more of a debt to hers than I like to recognize now. In the spring of 1950, a letter from a fan drew her attention to a series of books by a successful romantic novelist, who, said the fan, seemed to have been absorbing her work to some purpose, borrowing incidents, phrases and even names with a lavish hand. When Georgette Heyer read the books in question, she found so obvious a debt to her own work that she seriously considered filing a suit for plagiarism. With her usual thoroughness, she went through the books and drew up a long list of verbal borrowings, and the way the imitator misused them. This is fascinating for the light it casts on her own passionate accuracy. Like many Heyer imitators, this plagiarist

Ladies in morning dress in a phaeton and two. The Grand Sophy bought herself a high-perch phaeton.

misused the Jane Austen phrase 'I collect', and got sartorial details wrong, dressing a hero in Hessian boots with his breeches. 'Hessians were worn with pantaloons, never with breeches,' explained the expert.

Summing up in a long letter to her legal adviser, Georgette Heyer wrote that the imitator owed her: 'What no self-respecting author should owe to another . . . Cheek by jowl with some piece of what I should call special knowledge (all of which I can point out in my books) one finds an anachronism so blatant as to show that [they] know rather less about the period than the average schoolchild, and certainly have never read enough contemporary literature to acquire the sudden bit of erudition that every now and then staggers the informed reader . . . There is a certain salacity which I find revolting, no sense of period, not a vestige of wit, and no ability to make a character "live". There is a melodramatic bias, but the copying of names, the similarity of situations, the descriptions of characters have been enough to make one impartial reader at least detect the imitations.'

After this lively and justified criticism Georgette Heyer went on to say she hoped for a public apology, and the withdrawal of the offending books, but the field of plagiarism is a heavily mined one, and in the end no action was taken. In fact, she thought the plagiarist knew the borrowing had been spotted: 'The horrible copies of my books ceased abruptly.'

The Grand Sophy came out in 1950 both in England and in the United States, where Putnam were disappointed with its sales. Commenting on this to Frere, Georgette Heyer said: 'Except that every penny counts, the cash involved is almost negligible. Putnam's only pay me £300 in advance, and, lately, the royalties have been barely perceptible. Incidentally, I have now had one letter from [her editor at Putnam] explaining that no one in the States is reading historical novels; and now I have one . . . explaining that very few persons now read detective novels. So one wonders what they *do* read in America.'

Every penny counted. In the winter of 1950 Richard was at Cambridge, 'grappling with a five-day scholarship examination', but he would go to the university whether he got a scholarship or not. He was 'certainly bookish', said his proud mother, and had been 'the Finest Head of House . . . in years' at Marlborough. But public school and university are not cheap and the tax man was after her again. 'Sophy is selling between 400 and 500 copies a day. This spells RUIN!' she said, and wrote two books in 1950, trying a detective story for the first time since *Penhallow*. She sent *Duplicate Death* to Frere in December: ' "Todgers," you perceive, "can do it." Herewith one Detective Novel, between 90,000 and 100,000 words. I think I have done better, but I know I have done worse; and I have little doubt that it will sell a treat. Ronald has been carefully through it, to make sure that I have dropped the requisite clues; and he has OK'd it. I hope you'll like it. You have never read Miss Heyer's Masterpieces of Detection, so I must inform you that Hemingway is a well-known figure to my Fans. When I last wrote of him he was an Inspector, but Tony Hawke,[1] who badgered me for this book, says he is now a Chief Inspector. So I dutifully made him one.'

A significant dedication to *Duplicate Death* reads: 'This book having been written in response to the representation of certain members of the Bench and Bar is therefore dedicated to them with the Author's humble duty.' It is a useful reminder that men as well as women read Georgette Heyer, and not just the detective stories. Lord Justice Somervell bequeathed his Georgette Heyer collection to the library of the Inner Temple Bench, an unusual accolade for a romantic novelist.

Georgette Heyer would probably have been less dutiful about *Duplicate Death* if it had been one of her Regency comedies, but it is a readable book, with a clever punning title. The murder takes place during an evening of duplicate bridge and the original murder, by strangulation with a bit of picture wire, is duplicated by a second murder, thus causing Chief Inspector Hemingway a good deal of trouble. There is an engaging aristocratic heroine in disguise and one of Georgette Heyer's barrister heroes who is visited by Hemingway in his chambers:

> A comfortable room, overlooking the garden, which smelt of tobacco and leather, and was lined with book-shelves . . . An aged Persian rug covered most of the floor, and a large knee-hole desk stood in the window. Young Mr Harte . . . was sitting at this . . . glancing through a set of papers, modestly priced on the covering sheet at 2 guineas . . .

Before he can sit down, Hemingway removes '*The Times*, a paperbacked novel, a box of matches, two bundles of papers tied up with red tape, and a black cat' from a deep chair. The

1 An eminent legal friend.

chambers are attractive and the fee of two guineas significant. If this was the kind of fee Ronald could command, it is not surprising that every penny his wife earned counted. Unfortunately, Putnam, who had been publishing the historical novels steadily since *Friday's Child*, turned down *Duplicate Death* and Heinemann found the booksellers lukewarm about it. Georgette Heyer wrote gloomily to Frere that she was 'prepared for D. Death to flop badly here and for you to have a nervous breakdown upon reading the Q.G. If the price of gas doesn't go up, I shall put my head in the oven.'

But the printing of 70,250 for *The Quiet Gentleman* as against 34,500 for *Duplicate Death* shows that Heinemann did not share her gloom. Both books came out in 1951 and the sales of *Duplicate Death* were encouraging enough for her and Frere to begin to consider getting the rights in her previous detective stories back from Longman and Hodder and reprinting them. This proved to be a difficult business. Georgette Heyer had been becoming increasingly impatient with her agents, Christy & Moore, who had always acted for her. Leonard P. Moore had been a friend of her father's and she had dedicated *Helen* to him in 1928, calling him her 'friend Leonard P. Moore', but he was getting old now, and the relationship had gone wrong. She wrote impatiently: 'When you've known a man of his age since you were nineteen, and he *still* looks on you as a struggling young author, the situation is apt to be difficult. Having enjoyed the disadvantage of an Upbringing, I *cannot* be rude to old men!'

The Christy & Moore offices had been wrecked during the blitz, and Moore had moved out to his home in Gerrards Cross and refused to come back when the war was over. Georgette Heyer quite rightly thought that an agent's place is in the centre of things. And Moore had perhaps taken too literally her insistence that she be left alone, and had also yielded too easily to her refusal to consider what she thought the vulgar phenomenon of paperbacking when it first developed. She was later to blame him for this. As he grew older, he spent less and less time in the office and an atmosphere of muddle and divided

Little Sanctuary, Tothill Fields. Visiting her brother in this debtors' refuge Arabella encountered Leaky Peg and Quartern Sue. Georgette Heyer could describe poverty when she wanted to.

command developed there. As if that was not bad enough, he did not get on particularly well with Frere and, in Georgette Heyer's view, was altogether too close to Hodder & Stoughton. But the difference between them went further back than this. Moore had warned against the outright sale of the three titles to Heinemann in 1940, and been right; now he was against her accountant's scheme to form a limited liability company in an effort to lessen her tax bills. His representation in the United States was weak during the war years and he was becoming slow and obstructive. In the end, she lost patience with him in the autumn of 1951, and gave notice that she was leaving his agency and putting her affairs in Heinemann's hands for the future.

His reaction infuriated her: 'As for the implication that my work was more or less in my father's hands, and that he and Moore just settled things between them "for the poor child", it makes me seethe with fury! Enough to make my father haunt Moore, too! Rest assured, I was *not* encouraged to be weak-minded, nor had my father any real parental instinct! I adored him, but he was far more like a brother than a father.'

She asked Louisa Callender of Heinemann to take over the handling of her affairs, and invited her to come to lunch and discuss them: 'Not just at the moment, because my time is taken up with my Mamma, who is in a Nursing Home, but when I am able to draw breath again. There are all sorts of ramifications to my affairs I shall have to explain to you, and I feel that if I give you a really *nice* lunch, I may be able to cozen you into really promising to do frightful things, like Dealing with Fan Mail.'

She and Louisa became good friends, and she was soon writing her lively letters in dialogue form, ending one: 'Louisa, you really must not go on wasting my time like this! If you think I have nothing better to do than to sit here inexpertly typing letters to you, you much mistake the matter: I have to Jug a Hare. What? Write a BOOK? You are confusing me with someone else, Woman: I don't write books!'

Her affairs must have been quite a proposition for a busy woman to take on. The tax man has always been hard on authors, whose irregular earnings do not fit into a pattern set up for businessmen. One way of avoiding penal taxation is to form a limited liability company – paying oneself a salary, and one's family directors' fees, and Georgette Heyer did this at this time, forming a company called Heron Enterprises, which was administered by her accountant. There were inevitable risks of confusion about this, since Heron Enterprises were only responsible for titles from then on, the previous ones having still to be extricated from Christy & Moore, Longman and Hodder. Then there was the question of foreign royalties, which were paid direct to Mrs Heyer, with the exception of American ones. Louisa Callender soon decided that the whole administration of

86

the Heyer literary estate would be too much for her. In January 1952 she arranged a lunch at the Ivy for Georgette Heyer to meet Joyce Weiner, a literary agent who agreed to take over the handling of foreign and serial rights, and began a long and friendly relationship with her new author. She remembers her as an ideal client and good friend, totally businesslike and helpful, but also totally demanding: She Who Must Be Obeyed. She demanded and got priority. As well she might. She preferred to deal direct with her English publishers, which meant that there was no single professional eye on what was now an enormous literary estate.

The Quiet Gentleman came out in the autumn of 1951 and drew some criticisms that irritated Georgette Heyer: 'Have you seen the positive spate of letters from Clever Persons, pointing out how illiterate I am to talk of sons-in-law when I mean stepson? . . . mark how a rough answer shall impress an Illiterate Fan! My answers have been very rough indeed – and what is the outcome? I have a cringing letter thanking me for my Charming One! I . . . pointed out . . . that although my refusal to alter in-law to step might lay me open to the criticism of SOME, an emendation would draw down upon me the far more important strictures of OTHERS who would accuse me (rightly) of having introduced modern terminology into a Regency book.' She was not, in fact, on quite such sound ground as she thought. *The Oxford English Dictionary* does give her usage of mother-in-law for stepmother, but Dr Johnson does not, giving seven instances of the use of stepmother for this relationship.

Georgette Heyer was having trouble with her teeth that autumn and perhaps it shortened her temper. In the same letter she speaks of a *Daily Telegraph* review: 'Why does John Be – well I can't spell his alien name . . . hate my guts? He says my picture of Regency England is no more like the Real thing than he is like Queen Anne. He best knows whether he is like Queen Anne, but what the hell does he know about the Regency?'

Criticism of her private world always infuriated her, but there was right on both sides here. Her Regency world is a very carefully selected, highly artificial one. Reading her books, one remembers with surprise that the post-Waterloo years in which many of them are set were ones of appalling depression and poverty in England, with ex-servicemen begging in the streets and a very real danger of revolution. But then, the upper class of which she writes tended to ignore this too. To criticize her for not writing about the poor is like attacking Jane Austen for failing to mention the Napoleonic War. And, in fact, like Jane Austen in *Mansfield Park*, Georgette Heyer does occasionally look below the smiling surface of things. The Duke of Sale falls among thieves in *The Foundling*, and Arabella finds her brother in hiding in a very low back slum indeed in Tothill Fields.

The Quiet Gentleman has some of Georgette Heyer's liveliest lower-class slang, translated for the reader when necessary. A Bow Street Runner has been introduced into Stanyon improbably disguised as a gentleman's gentleman, and meets the Earl in the gallery:

'Getting me bearings, me lord,' explained Mr Leek. 'Which ain't as easy as anyone might think which was reared in this Castle! What I *do* say, and will stand to, is that I never in all my puff see a ken which I'd liefer mill! That is, *if* I *was* a mill-ken, which, o'course, I ain't. But there are them as I know as would slum this ken – ah, quicker than wipe your eye!'

'Break into it?' asked the Earl.

'Ah!' said Mr Leek. 'Well, look at them jiggers and glazes, me lord!'

'I beg your pardon?'

'What I *should* say,' Mr Leek corrected himself . . . 'is them doors and winders, me lord! Any prig could open 'em, and no one a ha'porth the wiser!'

A fan found *The Quiet Gentleman* disappointing and wrote to ask if Georgette Heyer was 'older and sadder and depressed'. It is indeed a quieter book than *The Grand Sophy* and may have disappointed the more simple-minded fans because it shows

Georgette Heyer once again enjoying playing hob with her own conventions. The spoilt young beauty is not the heroine after all; that part is played by plain, practical Drusilla, of whom both the reader and the hero grow increasingly fond. Like Sophy, Drusilla finds the male point of honour a sufficiently ridiculous business, and she is another heroine who will endear herself to feminists: 'Try as I will, I *cannot* be romantic,' she apologizes at last to the hero.

His eyes danced. 'Oh, I forbid you to try! Your practical observations, my absurd robin, are the delight of my life!'

Miss Morville looked at him. Then, with a deep sigh, she laid her hand in his. But what she said was: 'You must mean a sparrow!'

'I will not allow you to dictate to me, now or ever, Miss Morville! I mean a robin!' said the Earl firmly, lifting her hand to his lips.

Miss Morville's mother is an author of improving books, like Maria Edgeworth or Mary Wollstonecraft. Georgette Heyer had moved on from the letters and diaries of the late eighteenth and early nineteenth century to the novel and poetry. And she had been re-reading Jane Austen. This book is full of Austen echoes, including the dreadful Dowager who says she 'should have ridden very well, had I taken to it, for I should have had the benefit of my father's teaching'. Marianne Bolderwood owes her name to Marianne Dashwood, but some of her behaviour to a less attractive Jane Austen young lady. Patiently playing spillikins with the children on a hint from their grandmother, she is Lucy Steele with a difference.

The business of getting back the rights in the detective stories dragged on well into 1952, and Georgette Heyer grew increasingly impatient with both Christy & Moore and Hodder & Stoughton. The easiest and most considerate of people to deal with normally, she became formidable when roused, and most particularly if she thought advantage was being taken of her.

Finally she wrote a firm letter to Hodder in January 1952 asking for her rights back: 'I wish no publisher to print my books at the pistol's mouth.'

Sending a copy of this letter to Louisa Callender, she wrote: 'Here for the archives, is this Flower from my pen. I don't know why my infernal machine chose to slip a cog on the carbons: it All Goes to Show that I need a new one. O God, how I need one – ! Noiseless, and electrically driven, thank you very much. If Joyce Weiner would only sell a film right, blimey I'd blue about £150 on such a treasure! . . . I am wearing straw in my hair, and discover in myself a tendency to mow and gibber. No sooner do I get the gleam of an idea than my only remaining parent faints in the middle of the Cromwell road, and once more takes to her bed. Whither is fled the visionary gleam? Where is it fled, the glory and the dream? I wouldn't know, any more than the late Mr Wordsworth.'

Her life was full of distractions. Richard had got an exhibition to Pembroke College, Cambridge, but was doing his military service before he went up, and she described a 'week of ceaseless parties, Richard being home on embarkation-leave'. A less pleasant distraction was a threatened libel action by a solicitor whose six-letter name she had accidentally used for a not particularly attractive character who made a minor appearance on two pages of *Duplicate Death*. The real solicitor began by asking for a donation to charity but settled for an apology and the change of his name in future editions. Rejecting Heinemann's suggestions of Denoel, Eltons or Lundum, Georgette Heyer searched in vain for a six-letter substitute and in the end the name went unchanged. Names were important to her. She kept files of Christian and surnames, noting where she had used them; later in her life, when her friend Donald Sinden suggested a romantic story about some ancestors of his, to be called 'The Hodges of Warehorne', she rejected the idea: 'Such a common name; I couldn't use that.' Place-names were always safe; they would not involve her in libel actions.

As if she did not have problems enough, the cleaning woman

she had had since they moved to Albany suddenly left: 'The latest Aid to Writing a Bright Romance is the leaving without notice of my Daily Obliger, thank you very much. After more than nine years! Just walked out on me! No disagreement, or any unpleasantness whatsoever. How right my grandmother was when she laid it down as a maxim that Domestic Servants were a class by themselves, and Scum of the Earth! So all this week I have been wrestling with housework . . . Let me tell you (for my Biography) that neither by training nor by temperament am I suited to Domesticity.'

In fact, she usually got on very well with people who worked for her, and when her two Watkins aunts refused on snobbish grounds to go to the funeral of their own devoted servant, she and her mother made a point of going in their place. But it must have been maddening to have to turn to housework when she was hard at work on one of her most entertaining books. First called *Quadrille* and then *Chicken Hazard*, it ended up as *Cotillion*: 'Parts of it are rather good, and my dear Freddy is a poppet.' She ended this letter in characteristic style: 'Now, look here, Louisa, I've no doubt you think I have nothing better to do than to go on writing to you about nothing in particular, but you are the more mistaken. I have left Miss Charing at Grafton House, buying silk stockings at 12/- the pair (*c.p.* Letters of Jane Austen) and she must be rescued.'

This was one of the books where she began with a general outline, rather than a complete plot, for she told Louisa that: 'Having got my heroine to London, I now sit and wonder what happens *now*!' She finished half the book by March and sent it to Louisa with a brief outline of the second half and the proviso that she would not care 'to be bound down to a hard and fast pattern, for at any moment a new and still more absurd situation might present itself to me.' She was justifiably pleased with 'a very choice number called Lord Dolphinton' and remarked that 'the Pseudo-Heyer Hero hasn't yet appeared, but he has had a nice build-up.' She was teasing her fans again by making ineffective Freddy the hero rather than handsome Jack Westruther. The

Walking dress, 1805.

plot resembles that of *Friday's Child* except that it begins with an engagement rather than a marriage, which leaves the way open for a climax even funnier and more complex than that of *The Grand Sophy*. If she was really in doubt, half way through, about what was going to happen next, it cannot have been for long.

This is one of the tightly plotted conclusions that make one wonder why she never tried her hand at a play.

She finished *Cotillion* at her usual breakneck speed, despite a bad attack of sinusitis: 'It doesn't seem to stop me being quite humorous in *Cotillion*, so probably I *am* one of those people like Keats and Bizet, who flourish under adversity, after all. Or maybe it's just due to Dexedrine, with which (and gin, of course) I keep myself going . . . I finished the thing at 3.00 a.m. today, and I feel like hell. I am next going to perpetrate one, and if possible two, shorts, because my elder brother has announced his intention of getting married within a few months. A moment's reflection, my dear Louisa, will show you that this is NOT a non sequitur.'

One of the two shorts was 'Pink Domino'. She did not think very highly of her short stories. Sending a batch of them to Louisa Callender in 1951 she wrote: 'I think the best of the stories are "Snowdrift", "Pistols for Two", and "Hazard". You will find them all rotten, and exactly the same. I have another . . . "Full Moon", sold for £100 to W's Journal, July, 1948 . . . I think this wasn't bad, but I can't find it. The only other one is "Pursuit", which I wrote for the Queen's Book of the Red Cross.'

She looked on her short stories, even more than her detective books, as frank pot boilers. The new batch would pay for her brother Boris's wedding, which took place in the Albany chambers in July. She had an understanding with Heinemann that they held the advance payments for her books until she asked for them, and she wrote in July to ask for the £3,000 advance for *Cotillion*. She had received 'a hideous PAYE demand of £1,200 and a three figure dentist's bill for a new lower plate', and, finally, 'I have this day married off my little brother Boris, from these premises, and at some expense . . .'

Once 'the wedding-stuff' was behind her, she meant to get back to *Detection Unlimited* and also 'this accursed short story for *Good Housekeeping*' who had asked for one for their Coronation number. She had dedicated *Cotillion* to her old friend Carola Oman's husband, Sir Gerald Lenanton, who died in November.

Fencing at Mr O'Shaunessy's Rooms in St James's Street, by Cruikshank.
A favourite resort for would-be duellists like George Wrotham in Friday's
Child.

She wrote to Frere to ask if the words 'In affectionate memory'
could be added to the dedication. 'R and I are feeling pretty
shattered – not only for Carola, but on our own account. Gerald
was one of the nicest people we ever knew, and we shall miss him
horribly . . . *why* is it always the best people who die young, and
never the total losses?' Was she remembering her father? Their
circle of friends had always been small and close enough for any
diminution in it to be strongly felt. She had more or less lost
touch with her Heyer relations by now, and Joanna Pullein-
Thompson, the third of the trio who used to meet in Wimbledon
and talk books, had also drifted away. She had opted for a
comfortable unpretentious country life style, with ponies for the
children, while Georgette Heyer chose elegance, and Albany.
Josephine Pullein-Thompson, Georgette Heyer's god-daughter,
remembers one occasion when her godmother surveyed a rather
nursery-type lunch and announced that she *never* ate jelly, and
though she gave her lavish presents, she never pretended to like
girls, saying, 'Thank God I never had a daughter.' She was
perhaps too busy perfecting her own life style at this time to

accommodate herself to other people's different ones. But she always had time for her friends. When a school friend of Frank's whom they had known at Horsham sent his first book for her criticism, she gave it to him professionally as always and was amazed and alarmed to have all her advice taken. He was Christopher Landon, known as Kipper to his friends, and the book was *A Flag in the City*, a wartime thriller well grounded in personal experience. Published by Heinemann in 1953, it was the precursor of his best-selling *Ice-Cold in Alex*. But he was another of her friends who died young.

In the early 1950s, before things had got too bad between her and Christy & Moore, a new young recruit to the agency called John Smith was sent to call on Georgette Heyer, and remembers the occasion vividly. He was terrified of the agency's star author and daunted by the bleak approach to the chambers but once through the mahogany front door he met a warm welcome from the tall, shy lady who must, he felt, have an upper-class background and a good degree. The chambers suggested the town quarters of a county or academic family, and his hostess took pleasure in showing him her mahogany-furnished drawing-room and impressive book-lined study. Entertaining him with friendly gossip about the other celebrities who lived in Albany, she also talked in depth and with enthusiasm about her serious historical project, the great historical novel which was going to stun everybody. A distinguished lady rather than a handsome woman, she gave a slightly masculine impression, a commanding figure in a dark, square-shouldered suit. Recognizing the warm-hearted woman, shy and insecure behind the confident mask, he admired her style both in her life and her work, and divined her silent regret that this was something the reviewers failed to recognize. He would have agreed with the critic St John Ervine who, she remembered with pleasure, had once written about her 'seemly English'. But Ervine was one of the very few reviewers who noticed how passionately she searched for the right word as well as the accurate detail.

Chapter 5

*H*eron Enterprises was in trouble by 1953. Asking Heinemann for the advance on *Detection Unlimited* in June, Georgette Heyer wrote: 'Thanks largely to the antics of my accountant, my affairs are now in a chaotic state, my own account being overdrawn, and Heron's overweighted by a huge balance I dare not touch until the Commissioners of Inland Revenue (whom God assoil!) shall have decided a new Thing – of course against me.'

She hoped that *Detection Unlimited* would serialize, and when it was in fact rejected wrote: 'It is a great bore about the new thriller, and I can see the Bankruptcy Court looming. I can also see my mediaeval book fading into the far distance. I must think out a Typical Heyer Romance for instant sale.'

She and Ronald had been holidaying in Marlborough, but were now off to Droitwich. 'Ronald has an Enquiry there, so we're taking him – nurse and chauffeur, so to speak!' Richard was out of the army and going up to Cambridge, so he was also able to accompany his parents on what was to be an almost annual holiday at Greywalls Hotel, Gullane, in Scotland not far from Edinburgh. A thriving barrister by now, Ronald Rougier had become a member of the select and expensive Honourable Company of Edinburgh Golfers, and Greywalls abutted on their Muirfield golf course. His wife wrote: 'Excellent weather, and nothing to do except walk round Muirfield golf-course, enjoying the view, and the prowess of my male appendages, and play Bridge.' It was a holiday that suited her. She disliked hot weather and enjoyed the bracing air of the seaside links and the enclosed world of a golfing hotel.

Greywalls was just right for the Rougiers. It had been designed as a gentleman golfer's holiday home by Lutyens, and his frequent collaborator Gertrude Jekyll had planned the elegantly symmetrical walled gardens. When the present owners inherited it after the Second World War they turned it into a hotel without losing the atmosphere of a gentleman's home. To go there is a little like paying a visit to a luxurious country house left over from between the wars. The atmosphere is formal, a little masculine, with all the comfort and service of a London club. Having discovered it, the Rougiers went back year after year, always to the same room, number one, with its view across the links to the Firth of Forth and the hills of Fife beyond. Reserved at first, they gradually found a group of golf and bridge-playing acquaintances who also came back each year. One American couple remember how they gradually unbent from their formidable distance and finally invited them for a surprisingly relaxed evening at Albany. Ronald played a rather bullying game of bridge, and his wife spent her days doing tapestry and *The Times* crossword puzzle, reading, knitting and writing letters. As usual, she kept behind the mask of Mrs Rougier. When someone asked her what she did she replied, 'I'm a scribbler of trivial romances.' And when an enthusiastic young fan was presented to her, she made it quite clear that this was not what she wanted on holiday. She was impressive, rather than elegant, in a correct coat and skirt by day and a dark grey dress at night. She could turn herself out with immense style when an occasion demanded it, but this was her holiday. She was Mrs Rougier, sitting quietly in the lounge like anyone else.

Cotillion and *Detection Unlimited* both came out in 1953, with printings of 63,000 and 37,000 respectively. She was still queen of mystery and suspense. The *Sunday Times* said she was 'second to none in her ability to make detective stories entertaining', and the *Daily Mail* called her 'the wittiest of detective story writers', but the print figures told their own tale. And, besides, Ronald, who had provided the intricate plot and abstruse legal background for *Detection Unlimited*, was busy now on his own account. This was to be the last of their collaborations.

She was reading detective stories herself at this time and had strong views about them. She wrote of John Dickson Carr, another Heinemann author: 'All I see is that he is very ingenious with his locked rooms, and when you've said that, you've said everything. I didn't think any fictitious detective could set my teeth on edge quite as badly as Miss Ngaio Marsh's creature, but I find I was mistaken.' She had tried a locked room murder of her own in *Envious Casca* in 1941 and may have been re-reading it at this time, since she had now got the rights in the early detective stories back from Longman and Hodder and she and Louisa Callender were planning the Heinemann reprints. Re-reading *Behold Here's Poison*, she wrote that she was 'agreeably surprised when I went through it again, and usually I have to take to my bed when I've had occasion to look at an Early Work.' She remembered with pleasure that Torquemada had reviewed *A Blunt Instrument* in the *Observer* and begun: 'This is the best, and – for want of a better adjective – the truest of Miss Heyer's detective novels.' 'I almost let it go to my head,' she concluded.

Louisa Callender had sent her what purported to be a complete list of her titles and she went through it, adding *These Old Shades* and *The Conqueror* and crossing out the ones she wanted suppressed: all four of the straight novels, and *Footsteps in the Dark*: 'They, with such horrors as *Simon the Coldheart*, etc. [which had also been omitted from the list] are going to be buried in decent oblivion. If I were you, I'd let *Footsteps* join them. This work, published simultaneously with my son on Feb 12th, 1932, was the first of my thrillers, and was perpetrated while I was, as any Regency character would have said, increasing. One husband and two ribald brothers all had fingers in it, and I do not claim it as a Major Work.'

Returning from Scotland in the autumn of 1953, she was soon at work on the typical Heyer romance she had promised, and sent Louisa Callender a detailed outline of *The Toll-Gate* in November.

Townsend, the famous Bow Street Runner. The Regency equivalent of Scotland Yard, Bow Street Runners with names like Stogumber and Gudgeon appear as butts in such thriller-type novels as The Talisman Ring, The Corinthian *and* The Toll-Gate.

By now her ambivalent relationship with Miss Sutherland of *Woman's Journal* was well established and this advance synopsis would be revised and passed to her so that she could save space in the magazine for the finished book, and there could be 'no excuse for putting off serialization for months and months'. The interesting thing about this synopsis is that in fact the book turned out to be quite different. Georgette Heyer warned Louisa: 'For God's sake don't commit me to anything except mammoth hero and heroine and the toll-gate! It may sound a bit nebulous to you, and I admit that there are lots of loose ends, but it'll work out in the end . . . Once I've settled the plot it won't take me more than two months to write, and probably less.'

The original plot starts with the huge hero at the toll-gate. She describes him as 'Fair, and (of course) handsome, and not very Heyer-hero, because definitely *nice*.' And goes on:

Well, this character, riding along at dusk – probably on his way to stay with a friend – comes to a toll-gate and can't get the gate-keeper to show himself. Finds this person in extremis, distracted wife in attendance, and takes over his duties for the rest of the night. (Now, whether he did this out of kindness, or because the gate-keeper had been Done to Death – which I *think* happened – there's a general air of Fear and Mystery, which naturally intrigues our gallant Captain – or Major – I can't tell you; but I incline to think the latter was the way it was.)

Next morning, bright and early, he has to go out (unshaved) to open the gate to none other than Our Heroine, Nell Stornaway . . . *Well*! Our Hero is struck all of a heap by Nell, and instantly decides to go on keeping the gate. And all sorts of things happen – though exactly what I don't know. I rather think Henry Stornaway is carrying on some highly improper and illegal business, but what it was I'm damned if I can discover . . . *Furthermore*, Our Hero, little though he knows it, has succeeded to *his* cousin's Earldom, said cousin having had an accident . . . Another cousin . . . having discovered (by means as yet unknown) where Our Hero is lurking, tries to do him in.

This is the part of the plot that got jettisoned, which explains the now irrelevant opening scene at the Earl of Saltash's dreadful betrothal party, with a whole group of characters who never appear again. Georgette Heyer once said herself that her books tended to open slowly, and by this time her readers were obviously used to her gradual focusing first on a scene and then on the people in it. With the exception of John Staple's mother and sister, the group of guests are very lightly sketched in, and there is nothing memorable about the intended villain, Lucius

Staple, John's 'jovial but wicked' cousin. Georgette Heyer meant to go back and rewrite this scene, but never did.

This was a bad autumn for her. She was suffering from sinusitis, which interrupted the steady flow of her writing, and there were family problems too. One of the aged Watkins aunts first had a stroke, then fell down and broke her femur and was whisked against her will into the London Clinic. Mrs Heyer, 'seventy-eight and with a weak heart', was looking after her sister's affairs, and Georgette Heyer was busy writing letters and answering telephone calls. 'This sort of thing isn't really conducive to a flow of inspiration, but I'm carrying on (brave little woman), and the Home Critics assure me it's going like a breeze.'

Ronald had brilliantly solved the problem of the 'highly improper and illegal business' which Henry Stornaway was engaged in: 'Having a pachydermaton's memory he recalled, out of the blue, that I once read him a long spiel about coinage after Waterloo, when for the first time in years, we issued new gold and silver coins, and – which is important – minted the first sovereigns and half sovereigns, calling in the guineas.'

The nefarious business would be the theft of a consignment of the new sovereigns on their way to Scotland. With this settled, an agreed synopsis was sent off to Miss Sutherland, who protested about the way the villainous cousin disappeared after the first scene and did not surface until the very end. She also wanted to delay serialization so that the hardback would not be able to come out until October.

Georgette Heyer would have none of this. She could not, she said, afford the delay: 'My object in having written *Toll-Gate* was to get ahead of myself (so to speak) so that I could with a quiet mind return to my big mediaeval book for the best part of next year. To do that I must make sure of royalties rolling in steadily.'

If Miss Sutherland would not publish in time to allow summer hardback publication, she could not publish at all. In the end, Miss Sutherland agreed to serialize early enough to make July publication possible, and, in return, Georgette Heyer undertook 'to meet *her* wishes with regard to the story itself. I have eliminated the succession, and the wicked cousin, and have reduced the book to more reasonable proportions.' She ended by thanking Louisa 'for fighting this battle so successfully! Do you ever wish you had taken up cooking, or charring, or, in fact anything other than dealing with Authors?' The Rougiers were going to Rye for Christmas: 'Golf for the Boys and a Rest for Mother!' She must have been ready for it. But she never did revise the opening scene of *The Toll-Gate*.

Her letters about the financial planning that would enable her to get back to her mediaeval book have some interesting side-lights on her relations with Putnam, who had gone on publishing the historical novels after turning down *Duplicate Death*. Talking about the unlikelihood of her mediaeval book's proving suitable for serialization, she went on: 'I don't expect to sell it in huge quantities in this country, though there is a distinct possibility that I might do so in the United States. Purdy [of Putnam's] badgers me about it in every letter . . . and I know that the Yanks have just discovered the Middle Ages – but I'm not banking on any American sale, not having been born yesterday, but 51 years ago . . . The royalties I get from Putnam's are negligible.'

A few weeks later she wrote that Purdy planned to publish *The Toll-Gate* in the autumn: '. . . but wishes it were my mediaeval book. To an English author this seems cock-eyed, for one of our maxims is that the Great B.P. does not, and cannot, visualize Armour. I hope, however, to get down to this work again now that the future has been nicely arranged. You'd better start saving up paper, for I should think it would run to several million words!' But the mediaeval book was to be unlucky again. Writing in January to thank Louisa Callender for various items of good news about book-clubbing of her titles, Georgette Heyer reported more trouble with the Inland Revenue. Owing to bad advice, she had drawn more money from Heron Enterprises than she should have. The tax inspector claimed that these sums were undisclosed dividends, and she might find herself liable to an extra tax of some £3,000, news which appalled her. These were vast sums then. Probably as a logical result of this, she had an idea for:

A quick thriller – a *real* thriller, this time! I suddenly thought I might do something with the Ghost Squad of Scotland Yard, and have an incredibly sinister hero, looking like a thug and a crook all the way through . . . He shall be called Larry, which is a name eminently suited to a man who might be a crook, and I'll give him a nice nickname, and a scarred face; litter corpses about the place; make everyone talk at least three chapters ahead in a mystifying way; and do what lies in my power to suppress my own cramping sense of the Probable! *And* clutter up the plot with the sort of Nice Girl who gets into all the jams nice girls *don't* get into, and of course falls in love with Gangster-hero. Need I say that so far from disclosing his pure white soul, he ties her up and gags her at a crucial moment – I can't at the moment imagine why, but don't you worry! I shall think up a good reason!

This will not be a Noble Work, but it might be a good serial, and it might find an American publisher. If I do it, I shall do it at once, hoping to polish it off by March – after which I shall retire into the Middle Ages, and be no trouble to anyone for months.

She never did write this book, which was probably just as well, as the plot shows a considerable similarity to that of *Footsteps in the Dark* and she was obviously far from serious about it. The synopsis reads dangerously like a send-up of the contemporary romantic thriller. In fact, she was trying her hand in a new and highly respectable sphere that winter, perhaps as a possible alternative to the detective stories. She was writing short essays or articles, and Punch published two of them, 'Books about the Brontës' on 31 March and 'How to be a Literary Critic' on 28 April. Five others that failed to get published survive in typescript. They are: 'Mr Rochester', 'Barabbas', 'Fathers', and 'Ideal State, I & II'. Sharp and entertaining, they are written in stylish unmistakable Heyer prose. 'How to be a Literary Critic' and 'Barabbas' are particularly interesting as giving her views on critics and publishers. She thought nothing of critics. Addressing herself to the would-be critic, she says:

> If, when you are first handed the latest work of one whom you suspect to be your literary superior, you feel that it would be effrontery for you to criticize it, do not decline to do so. Remember that no qualifications are necessary for a Literary Critic, and that this is the Day of the Little Man, when the more insignificant you are, and the more valueless your opinions, the greater will be your chance of obtaining a hearing.

She returns to this theme in 'Ideal State, I & II', which are an ironic discussion of the best way to achieve a state of universal mental torpor. Reading must be discouraged, since it is 'an exercise disastrously conducive to Thought'. It is quite enough if a man can read forms, and he 'must be able to write, so that he can Fill in Forms'. Aside from this necessary function, he should be encouraged to take in information only in the easiest ways, in comic strips or by radio and television, from which 'anything tending to make Man doubt the intrinsic excellence of Mediocrity ought to be suppressed'. It is just as well that Georgette Heyer did not survive into the age of the video cassette. 'On no account,' she wrote savagely, 'should the man of Ideas be allowed to contaminate the Masses.'

'Barabbas' shows her kinder to publishers than to critics, and with cause. It was written at the time of one of the periodic battles between publishers and authors as to the publishers' right to percentages of outside sales, and she ends by coming down on the side of the publisher. 'I think I won't go against him. At any rate, not until I've discovered how to dispense with his services altogether.'

This article has some interesting sidelights on her own career:

I am not one of those Authors who are so inundated with offers from Film-Producers, and the BBC, that they count on such sales as integral parts of their income. I've never regarded them as anything more than the lucky bets I made; and if my publisher had wanted a share of the winnings I shouldn't have recognized the gross injustice of such a claim.

A considerate author herself, she could see her publisher's point of view, and wrote with her habitual irony:

I'm not going to waste any more pity on him for being obliged to listen to my Life-story, to my opinion of my own worth, and to Good Bits from my new novel. If he's so keen on books he ought to enjoy such sessions, just as he ought to welcome the arrival, at his private address, on Saturday afternoon of the first six chapters of my new novel, scrawled all over with illegible emendations, typed with a ribbon which might, with advantage, have been changed a month ago, and accompanied by an urgent request that he should read it over the weekend, and let me know his candid opinion of it first thing on Monday. If he's fool enough to do more than glance at the thing, he doesn't know his job; and if he favours me with his candid opinion, he's a case for the Relieving Officer.

'Mr Rochester' shows her thinking about her craft:

It is an accepted fact that women form the bulk of the novel-reading public, and what woman with romantic leanings wants to read novels which have as their heroes the sort of men she meets every day of her mundane life? Charlotte [Brontë] knew, perhaps instinctively, how to create a hero who would appeal to women throughout the ages, and to her must all succeeding romantic novelists acknowledge their indebtedness. For Mr Rochester was the first, and the Nonpareil, of his type. He is the rugged and dominant male, who yet can be handled by quite an ordinary female: as it might be, *oneself.* He is rude, overbearing, and often a bounder; but these blemishes, however repulsive they may be in real life, can be made in the hands of a skilled novelist extremely attractive to many women. Charlotte Brontë, immensely skilled, knew just where to draw the line. She doesn't allow Mr Rochester's rudeness to take the form of unendearing vulgarity, any more than she permits his libertine propensities to show themselves, except in retrospect.

And, on his appearance:

> She had the genius to state that he was not a handsome man, thus lifting him out of the ordinary run of heroes. What, in fact, did this ugly hero look like? Had he a squint, or a harelip? Charlotte knew her job better than that! 'He had a dark face, with stern features and a heavy brow.' Promising we think, already a little thrilled. But what were his defects? We learn that he had a chest too broad for his height, and find nothing to disgust us in this. Nor is it long before we read of his 'colourless, olive face, square, massive brow, broad and jetty eyebrows, deep eyes, strong features, firm, grim mouth – all energy, decision, will,' and like Jane, we succumb to this splendid creature.

Mr Rochester is, of course, the original of the Heyer hero, Mark I, and it is good to see Georgette Heyer so totally aware of this herself. She was every inch the professional craftswoman. But only two of this batch of short pieces got published. Did her name as a romantic novelist militate against her in this field? It seems extremely likely, and must have been maddening for her. Aside from anything else, these were some of her very rare rejection slips, an unpleasant surprise for someone who had been published 'first crack out of the bag' at nineteen. She had had books turned down for serialization and in America, but for her America did not really count. It was one thing to write *Penhallow* as a contract breaker, intending Hodder to turn it down, quite another to have her articles returned to her.

The Toll-Gate came out in July 1954, its publication celebrated by 'Georgette Heyer Week' in bookshops in England, Australia, and South Africa. All was going well with this aspect of her work and she was already planning another Regency romance:

> Which I may well call *Bath Tangle*. It is all about the Lady Serena Carlow, only child of the Earl of Spenborough, deceased immediately before the book starts; and Ivo, Marquis of Rockingham, *to* whom she was once betrothed, *with* whom she quarrels on the smallest provocation, and who (to her wrath) is left Trustee to her fortune. He is *very* Heyer-hero. Opening chapter – in case [Miss Sutherland] wants to set the artist to work at once – is at the Family Seat, Serena and her very young stepmother, Emily [Fanny], discovered awaiting return of Funeral Party, for the reading of the Will. Serena about 25, queenly, beautiful, and red-headed; Emily [Fanny], a diaphanous and appealing blonde. (They have to be like that, so that each can look terrific in mourning. Emily [Fanny], being a matron, would wear a cap, with black ribbons. Serena not.)

There writes the totally professional author, and the rest of the synopsis, this time, is an almost exact description of the book, except that Georgette Heyer discovered with horror, when half way through, that her hero's name, Rockingham, was that of a little-known English Prime Minister. After considerable heart searching, she changed it to Rotherham. She cared a great deal about names, and the way they ran in her elegant prose.

The novelist A. S. Byatt called this a tired book in her *Sunday Times* article, and it does revert to situations and characters Georgette Heyer had used before. Serena owes a great deal to Lady Barbara in *An Infamous Army* and Rotherham is every inch the Heyer hero. It is interesting to compare him with Ravenscar in *Faro's Daughter*. The essays show that Georgette Heyer had been re-reading the Brontës, and Rotherham is even more of a

Rochester figure than Ravenscar, but he is also a very much more interesting character. Once again, the story is of the battle royal between strong-minded hero and heroine, but there is more to this one. Rotherham learns from Serena that even pride of birth can be excessive. And Serena, who has been brought up 'more as a son than a daughter' by her adoring father, loses not only a beloved companion by his death, but also the man's world she shared with him. Reduced to knotting fringe and sharing the tittle-tattle, gossiping life of Bath with her widowed stepmother, she shocks her staid new fiancé by driving her high-perch phaeton in Bath, and frightens him by suggesting he stand for Parliament. He wants to put his wife on a pedestal and have her keep quiet there; she wants a man to fight with. Neither of them realizes that he is falling in love with her white-mouse stepmother, and it is lucky for them both that Rotherham can be relied on to sweep like a gale through their lives. This is another book where a shared sense of humour is the bond between hero and heroine.

But it has less actual comedy than the previous books. Instead, there is an Austenlike irony in its treatment of the linked problems of snobbery and money. The toad-eating Lady Laleham turns out to have one of Georgette Heyer's best vulgarians for a mother. Mrs Floore is in the splendid tradition of Tom's terrible old pa in *The Foundling*, but where Mr Mamble the ironmaster was unrelievedly dreadful, we like Mrs Floore. This book is a watershed one. Before it, Georgette Heyer had sometimes played at turning the romantic conventions upside down; now she is beginning to look through them, and into the human heart. She herself called it a love story rather than an adventure story, and there are some interesting, unconscious echoes of *Instead of the Thorn*, the most feeling of her straight novels. The relationship between Rotherham and Fanny, to whom he engages himself when Serena takes her Major, is at once like and unlike that of the married hero and heroine in *Instead of the Thorn*. But Rotherham is intentionally frightening Emily off by a show of passion, and it is Serena whom he finally

Ball dress, 1810.

calls 'you beautiful bad-tempered thorn in my flesh'. There are unmistakable hints of autobiography in this book. Georgette Heyer, like Serena, had been brought up as her father's favourite and found in him, as she herself said, 'more a companion than a father'. And she, too, had undoubtedly encountered toad-eaters by now, and turned all the more in on herself because of them.

While she was busy with *Bath Tangle* in July 1954, *Everybody's* asked for a series of articles on a Regency subject, but Georgette Heyer refused. Publication in *Everybody's* was no substitute for publication in *Punch* and 'to finish *Bath Tangle* by the time I leave for Scotland will strain my powers to the limit of their endurance'. She was very tired, writing in another letter: 'I am continually astonished to perceive how smoothly it reads . . . for my head hasn't ceased to ring (like a dimly heard bell) for a fortnight.' She was indeed pushing herself to the limit of her powers.

She did finish *Bath Tangle* before they left for Greywalls in August, but took a copy with her and wrote Frere that she had re-read it and 'found it (like Old Mr Brontë) much better than likely . . . it won't be *my* fault if you don't sell large quantities of it. Though, of course, if you don't *advertise* properly . . . But you know the rest of that by heart!' This sounds a little like a quotation from 'Barabbas' and it is a rare author who has not said something of this kind to her publisher.

Georgette Heyer always enjoyed talking books with Frere: 'How do you like the assorted balls about the Death of the Novel, now cluttering up the columns of the *Observer*? It *would* be started by Harold Nicolson, I feel. So far the views of our leading novelists have not had an airing. Too busy raking in the shekels by *writing* novels, I assume . . . I perceive by Sunday's S. Times that W.S.M. [William Somerset Maugham] is all set to become senile about Emily Brontë. The trouble is that David Cecil has really said all there is to be said about the Victorian novelists, and in such crystal and lucid prose that it would be hard to better it. So far, in W.S.M.'s series, I have been quite awfully unimpressed. What do you think? Nothing new yet – and if the promised bombshell about Emily is the Lesbian angle, that was done in the worst book about her ever perpetrated.'

She returned to this subject in November: 'W.S.M. can hardly have been pleased by Rebecca West's devastating criticism in *Time & Tide*! A slight flavour of personal animosity, I thought – but how penetrating, how true. She *is* a good critic.'

The Rougiers had the decorators in. 'I am the merest housewife, and still in the throes of house-decoration.' Painting their double front doors, the men left them open to dry, but the maid, leaving, bolted one of them, making it impossible for Georgette Heyer to get in without smearing herself with paint. Describing this to Frere, she rewrote her favourite Lear limerick:

> There was an old man who supposed
> That the front door was partially closed;
> But some very large rats ate his boots[1] and his hats,
> While that futile old gentleman dozed.

Despite the decorators, she was in good spirits, and was entertained by a chance encounter with Miss Sutherland of *Woman's Journal* which she described to Louisa Callender: 'Did Frere tell you that I fell alive into the clutches of [Miss Sutherland]. It was really very funny, for both he and I were taken by surprise, and almost stunned by the shock. We had both imagined someone *quite* different to look at! He was giving me lunch at Quaglino's when one of the directors of A. Press[2] came in with two females, saw Frere, and came over to our table. Upon learning my identity, he begged permission to "present" someone who was "very anxious to meet me". And the next instant, there was [Miss Sutherland], looking rather like Cassius, only hungrier, bowing from the waist, and murmuring disjointed inaudibilities. All passed off with immense affability . . .' But there was no change in the two powerful ladies' relationship of armed neutrality.

1 'Coats' in the original.
2 Associated Press.

Chapter 6

*E*nvious Casca, the last of the reprinted detective stories, came out in 1955 as well as *Bath Tangle*, and once again the print figures are significant: 61,500 for *Bath Tangle* as against a mere 19,000 for *Envious Casca*, now reprinted for the first time since 1941. Georgette Heyer was hard at work on *Sprig Muslin*, writing in May: 'If I can turn out another bleeding romance by mid-July, I can get back to John without – I hope to God! – losing the thread.' She managed it, but there was trouble with Miss Sutherland over arrangements for serialization of *Sprig Muslin* and another bit of bad news when Louisa Callender left Heinemann. Georgette Heyer had been thinking about how the mediaeval book should be published, granted its great length, and wrote Frere: 'Did you ever see a woundy great novel by a bloke called Armstrong? God knows what its title was, but it was the dullest book I've ever tried to read – oh, *King Cotton*! and it stank! – Well, if Collins could bring *that* out in one volume, Someone Not a Hundred Miles from Here can damn well do the same by J. of L.' She had been reading about the bankruptcy proceedings against a fellow author, Vivyan Holland. 'Did you *see* the sums that I.R. filched from him, under every imaginable pretext? What made me feel really ill was Vivyan's statement that when his income went up, so did his expenditure. *And why not?* Oh, Christ, why did I have to be born into this *filthy* age?'

There was nothing egalitarian about Georgette Heyer. She thought the labourer worthy of her hire. Working hard, she

Evening dress, 1818.

expected to enjoy the fruits of her labours. She liked the elegances of life, earned them, and bought them. Their chambers were well, if sombrely, furnished; she dressed with impeccable and expensive taste, with a penchant for huge hats and the very best handbags and shoes. She bought her gulls' eggs at Harrods and her game pie at Fortnum's. She gave expensive and carefully chosen presents, a crocodile handbag or a gold watch ceremoniously presented to someone who had served her well. She liked to give delicious dinners for her close circle of friends, and her occasional parties were lavish. It all cost money. Her expenditure, like Vivyan Holland's, went up with her earnings. And why not?

Having finished *Sprig Muslin* she went to work with a will on the mediaeval book, but was anxious by now about her American publisher's attitude to it. Her editor at Putnam kept referring to it as her book about Joan of Arc, 'in spite of my repeated assurances that it is NOT a book about Joan of Arc'. She was 'thinking rather seriously of severing connections with Putnam's', and had 'no intention of letting them handle John of Lancaster. They have never succeeded in selling me in the States, and when they published *Bath Tangle* I consented to accept a lower advance.' She had now learnt that they had not even sold up to that advance. 'It seems to me that I may well be a drug on the American market. At the same time, I get good notices, and enthusiastic fan-letters . . . God forbid I should blame my own shortcomings on to my publisher, yet I can't feel, and never have felt, that Putnam's are much use.' In the end, she decided to let them have *Sprig Muslin* and then think again.

Sprig Muslin, which Georgette Heyer had described as 'another bleeding romance' is, in fact, one of her best books, combining the high comedy of the early ones with the deeper feeling that had begun to show in *The Quiet Gentleman* and *Bath Tangle*. Hester Theale is a quiet, plain heroine like Drusilla in *The Quiet Gentleman*, and even the knowledgeable reader may not spot her as the heroine at once. The plot is like that of *The Corinthian* and *The Foundling* in that it is based on an early, disastrous proposal, but this time Hester, stronger minded than Harriet in *The Foundling*, refuses Sir Gareth just because she loves him. Georgette Heyer is playing games with her fans again, offering runaway Amanda's romantic story, gently mocked, as counter-point to Sir Gareth's gradual falling in love with Hester. The concluding scenes show her writing at the top of her form, combining high comedy with strong feeling, and leave one with the kind of satisfaction one gets only from the very best, from a Shakespeare comedy or a Mozart opera. It is no wonder if she disliked having books like this one dismissed by the critics as 'another Georgette Heyer'. This time, she wrote Frere about one perceptive reviewer: 'The critic – a person of taste and discernment – says you want a touch of genius to produce my books.' And then, a highly characteristic note: 'No, no, not *you*, idiot! *ME*!'

Georgette Heyer is often accused of repeating herself, and *Sprig Muslin* is at once a classic case of this and a demonstration of how little it matters. Amanda and her Brigade-Major owe a great deal to Juana and hers in *The Spanish Bride*, while Amanda's relationship with the poet Hildebrand harks back to Pen Creed's with her childhood sweetheart in *The Corinthian* and Cecilia's with Augustus Fawnhope in *The Grand Sophy*. These are themes of Georgette Heyer's, used as a composer might, as Mozart, for instance, would use a theme from *Figaro* to make a point in *Don Giovanni*. In the world of high comedy, it is sometimes possible successfully to repeat a success.

Sprig Muslin came out in 1956, by which time Georgette Heyer had finished *April Lady* and was denigrating it as usual. Writing to comment on Heinemann's proposed blurb, she said: 'It almost sounds as if the book might be worth reading! . . . the way you've avoided the use of such words as *corny*, and *drivel* is just *too* wonderful! Of course, you've *implied* them in the first paragraph – and when I see the bare bones of the story set out, very fair-mindedly, I do feel that. I am sunk beneath reproach. I am now about to perpetrate another piece of nonsense so that for the first time in my life I shall have Something up my Sleeve. I rather want to call it *Snowbound*, but as I'm still uncertain about the plot this isn't yet decided. As a preliminary I've dug up a lot more Regency slang, some of it very good indeed, and the rest quite unprintable.'

Her own special brand of Regency language was one of the aspects of her private world that Georgette Heyer particularly enjoyed and she would not tolerate criticism of it. It is, of course,

The Channel Packet, by Rowlandson. Tom Orde could not get Lady Ingham to face it in Sylvester.

as highly selective and as artificial as the world she describes. A comparison with Jane Austen is illuminating. There is hardly a phrase in her dialogue that is not instantly comprehensible to the modern reader. Georgette Heyer, on the other hand, liked to load every rift with ore. This linguistic orgy, in narrative as well as dialogue, was one of the ways by which she distanced her private world from the real one. And, as the last quotation shows, it was a continuing delight to her. Her imitators, parroting her phrases, reduced them to cliché, but for her the language was a living thing. At the end of *April Lady*, the heroine, Nell, is being escorted home by her husband's cousin after meeting him in compromising circumstances. Unfortunately they encounter her brother Dysart and his friend Mr Fancot, both of them cheerful-drunk. Dysart tries to force a quarrel on Hethersett:

Nell laid a hand on his arm, and said: 'Dy, *pray* don't be so gooseish! You quite mistake the matter, you know! Indeed, it is abominable of you to think such horrid things, besides being excessively embarrassing!'

'Don't you try to bamboozle me!' replied her brother, shaking off her hand. 'Are you going to name your friends, sir, or are you not?'

'You wouldn't remember 'em if I did. What you need is a damper: you're as drunk as a brewer's horse!'

'Oh, no, I'm not! I'll tell you what *you* are! A damned loose fish! A regular hedge-bird! A man-milliner, by God! *Cowhearted*!'

Regency blades probably did not talk exactly like this, but Pierce Egan's *Life in London* shows that they did have their own language, for their own private world, just as Mayfair does today. And Georgette Heyer's version of it has the stamp of life, but life intensified.

Reading the proofs of *April Lady*, Georgette Heyer returned them to Frere with a note ending: 'Isn't it *nice* to listen to English batsmen making Australian bowlers look like three penn'orth of bad cheese?' She was a devoted spectator sportswoman and wise people did not ring her up when golf or the Test Match were going on. Another spectator sport she and Ronald enjoyed was horse-racing, which may have cost them money. Years later she would write, 'I am not a betting woman nowadays, but the National was always my lucky race.' *Snowbound* had become *Sylvester*, 'A VERY nice book this time, with a New Plot!' And her resident audience had grown. Richard was down from Cambridge and living at home. He had followed in his father's footsteps and been called to the Bar in 1956 and was working in Melford Stevenson's chambers. His devoted mother now enlivened her letters with descriptions of his progress and the headlined case of Bodkin Adams, the Eastbourne doctor who was accused of murdering his elderly patients. 'It makes Landru and Christy look like tyros,' she wrote, enjoying it all immensely. It must have seemed strange to have a beloved male beginning at the Bar again, after almost twenty years. They would be a family of three for a while yet. Friends describe Georgette Heyer as a devoted mother, but a formidable critic of her son's girl friends. Most mothers are.

April Lady returns to the theme of *The Convenient Marriage*, but here the hero and heroine are already married, and already at odds when the story opens. Like Harriet in *The Foundling*, Nell Cardross has been warned by her idiotic mother that hers is a marriage of convenience only; she must not expect love from her husband. So she has plunged into society, and debt, and her husband, who fell in love with her at first sight, is beginning to think he made a great mistake. A lively sub-plot deals with the affairs of his romantically-minded young sister, Letty, who is in love with a civil servant. Once again, the sub-plot mocks the romantic theme, which the main plot is seriously considering. Georgette Heyer usually stays outside her heroines' bedroom doors, but this book is an exception. Delicately, but unmistakably, as she did in *The Convenient Marriage*, she makes it clear that Nell and her husband have slept together, and that he is neglecting her since he became jealous. What he does not know is that his indiscreet sister has told Nell about the mistress he used to keep. She is jealous too, and the stage is set for a fine tangle of misunderstanding and one of Georgette Heyer's closely plotted conclusions.

But she seems to have been writing under even more pressure than usual at this time. An unusual bit of carelessness in *Sprig Muslin* is the double use of the name Ludlow. The hero is Sir Gareth Ludlow and Hildebrand is going to Ludlow on his walking tour. And *April Lady* has what she admitted as one of her rare errors. Jeremy Allandale, the civil servant Letty loves, is described as employed at the Foreign Office, and the *Times Literary Supplement* reviewer pointed out that a Foreign Office clerk would not have been posted Secretary to the Embassy in Brazil. 'I think the man is quite right,' Georgette Heyer wrote to

A dandy. This could be a portrait of Sir Nugent Fotherby in Sylvester.

Frere: 'I had even meant to look the point up, because Ronald queried it at the outset. And I'm damned if I know the answer. Rather erudite of the reviewer: Carola Oman hasn't said a word about it, and she would have, if she'd seen the error. The point in question was my having put Allandale, a diplomat, in the FO. The TLS speaks of him as a "clerk". I never said that, however. Left it purposely vague.' She did indeed. Allandale's position is indicated with the lightest of casual touches, the skilled professional very much in control.

1957 was 'not my lucky year'. There were three deaths in the Rougier family, one a close and immediate loss, all involving a great deal of work for Ronald. And the Inland Revenue had 'started on its pet sport' in January. 'They wrenched more than £11,000 from us last year . . . quite irrespective of our personal I.T. and Sur-Tax. I think Jamaica would be too hot a climate for me, but what about the Channel Islands? If I am going to be taxed on money I never so much as touched, because I.R. got there first, I think I'll either leave the country or go into liquidation, and not write any more books.' She did not mean it of course. She and Ronald would never for a moment have seriously considered becoming tax exiles, but they became almost paranoid about the tax man over the years. The unchartered firm of accountants who set up Heron Enterprises were successful neither in handling the company nor in explaining its intricacies to the Rougiers. The inevitable tax demands went on coming as unpleasant surprises, and since she associated so little with other authors, Georgette Heyer did not have the consolation of their horror stories about the problems of the author and the tax man.

She ended the letter about taxes: 'My Mama is 81 tomorrow, and if I thought I should live to anything approximating that age I would Take Steps right now.' And then, 'so saying, she went upstairs to fry some fish'. She would always take the wry, ironic line, but it was not a good winter. She came down with a throat infection which was finally diagnosed as a streptococcal throat, what Jane Austen would call 'a putrid sore throat', she said. It kept recurring, and, most unusually, she was typing 'laboriously, about half a page a day' of *Sylvester*. 'Foolish persons keep on urging me to go away for a Nice Rest, and a Change of Air; but only Ronald took No for an answer, understanding that to go away, leaving a book on the stocks, would fret me into my grave. There are times when I quite *like* that man.' *Sylvester* was running long and she could not decide whether to cut it or let it rip. In the end she cut it and was sorry afterwards. 'It could and should have been better. And it *was* better until I got cold feet, and cut out what wouldn't please the Fans.'

The weather was bad during their annual holiday at Greywalls. She suffered badly from a bee sting, then developed fibrositis and came back to London to begin what was to be a losing battle with overweight. She had never taken any exercise she could avoid, and never would. But Richard, 'now a fully

fledged barrister', was starting on a successful career, and his
mother told a friend that he had won the Profumo Cup for golf:
'played for yearly by the members of the Inner Temple (and to
be kept clean for a year, thank you!)' Writing to the old friend
who had been their landlady years before in Hove, she described
her mother's tendency to black out in the street: 'Twice have I
recovered her from a Casualty Ward!' And concluded, 'Still no
prospective daughter-in-law, though cohorts of attractive young
women. When they get married to other men, Richard dances at
their weddings, and a year later becomes a godfather!'

She did not like Heinemann's proposed blurb for *Sylvester*, and
provided an alternative, with an apologetic preamble: 'Without
wishing to sound insufferable, I don't think the Faithful Public
wants to know anything more than that it's the mixture as before.
So I have concocted a fresh blurb, based on yours. I am quite
unable to go into ecstasies about myself, but you can add (if you
feel you must!) what flattery may occur to you . . . What a ghastly
job it is, writing blurbs! It took me *hours*! I hope you think it will
do.' It is in fact one of her more pedestrian blurbs, failing to do
justice either to the comedy or the real feeling of *Sylvester*. Like
Bath Tangle this is a book about pride. Sylvester, Duke of Salford,
has been spoilt a little by his high rank, and now, deciding to
marry, assumes that any girl will be glad to have him. He learns
his mistake when plain Phoebe Marlow runs away rather than
receive his addresses. As he has decided not to offer for her, this
is disconcerting, but the discovery that she has caricatured him
ruthlessly in a romantic novel is still more so. Thrown together
in a series of comic-dramatic adventures, they find they share the
all-important sense of humour, but still the gulf between them
remains unbridgeable. In the end Sylvester's mother intervenes
and they fall into each other's arms at last, the physical contact
solving everything. Georgette Heyer may keep outside the
bedroom door but she is very much aware of the importance of
physical passion.

Sylvester has a group of splendid minor characters. Sylvester's
mother is a rarity for Georgette Heyer, an intelligent parent who

actually plays a constructive part in her child's story. Sir Nugent Fotherby is one of her best dandies, and Ianthe, his bride, a marvel of a silly woman who, eloping with Sir Nugent, 'had forgotten, in an orgy of expensive shopping, to provide for her son's needs'. And that son, Edmund, is a brilliantly drawn, engaging, bad little boy. The story moves with remarkable speed, achieved partly by the quick change of focus Georgette Heyer learnt from Jane Austen. We glance from the mind of one character to another almost without noticing we are doing so, as when Phoebe's arrival at Sylvester's town house, at the end of the book, is observed by his swarm of servants, all aware that 'his grace had chosen a leg-shackle at last'. The group of devoted servants, acting as chorus, is an integral part of Georgette Heyer's private world.

In the public one, her tax troubles got worse in 1958. Describing a new demand for over £4,000 she went on: 'And people are *afraid* of Russian missiles! Let 'em come! I for one am tired of an unequal struggle – and I am made violently unwell by the reflection that I am being forced to contribute towards a Welfare State of which I utterly Disapprove. The thought that I must also be contributing towards the expense of sending our Leading Chadband on a luxury Empire tour is almost too much for me!' Chadband, the pious, eloquent humbug of Dickens's *Bleak House*, was her name for Harold Macmillan, who was Prime Minister at the time, and not nearly Tory enough for the Rougiers. Her fury at tax demands that she did not understand was exacerbated by the conviction she shared with Ronald that their money was being used for all the wrong things.

Luckily, she had 'a fairly promising idea for the next book. A short one, I fancy, and not a lot of plot, but I like my heroine, and think the hero should please the fans . . . I'd like to call it *Venetia*.' Writing in January 1958 she hoped to have it done by April, 'barring such Acts of God as held me up over *Sylvester*'. By early March, she had done about 25,000 words and hoped to be finished by the end of the month. 'I think I should describe the book as a simple love-story – God knows what's come over me!

But it's useless to try to write a rather funny book if no funny character occurs to one. I never do my most sparkling stuff when labouring under adversity – and I don't deny that having, through ignorance of the questionable methods of the Treasury, reached an entirely false idea of what I owed this shoal of sharks, I feel more like Putting a Welcome Period to my existence than being witty . . . If this were a *real* Welfare State, a special and Large allowance would be made to people like me, for Housekeeping – because it would be recognized that a woman who writes romances which bring in large sums to the Treasury clearly can't be expected to waste time and energy on Household Thrift – and probably wouldn't be able to, even if she *had* the time.'

Her good friend Frere found a solution to her financial crisis and she wrote gratefully: 'Thank you for adding my stupid cares to your own. I feel very conscience-stricken about that. There are two sorts of people in the world: those to whom you take your success, and those to whom you take your failures – far less numerous . . . You belong to the second – and that is your misfortune, and Creatures like me trade on it. If you *could* pull off such a deal as you described it would ease things a lot, but *please* don't let my affairs become an infernal nuisance! If the worst came to the worst I could always offer to sell *Venetia* to you, lock, stock and barrel – to hell with it! . . . I do hope Miss Wallace [as Mrs Frere, Edgar Wallace's daughter, was affectionately called] is amended of her rheum? Give her my dear love, and tell her that I look forward to seeing her. Suggest to her that she gives me a ring when she comes up to town. It always does me good to exchange frivolities with her: she never says "How do you mean exactly?" Oh, tell her I've got a nice, bawdy story with which to sully her chaste ears! That'll bring her up to town, if I know her!' She had found a kindred intelligence in Mrs Frere, who remembers lunches full of laughter, not over personalities, and Georgette Heyer's stylish, elegantly turned phrases, her 'glittering Corinthianisms'. She talked about everything except her books, thinking what she called her 'fellow Inkies' a doleful lot.

Georgette Heyer with her good friends Mr and Mrs A. S. Frere at a Windmill Press garden party in the Forties. Georgette Heyer (centre) was mistaken, on this occasion, for Enid Bagnold, and thought it a great joke.

Venetia was running long and Miss Sutherland would have to cut it. 'Tell her that Barkis is willing – and that I don't think there should be any difficulty about it. This isn't an adventurous novel, nor is there any movement in it worth mentioning . . . I haven't yet read it through, but what I *have* read seemed to me not at all bad . . . Ronald seems to like it, and is kind enough to say that he doesn't think it's a bad thing that it's rather different from my

Countess Lieven waltzing at Almack's, by Cruikshank. Wife of the Russian Ambassador, she was one of the patronesses of Almack's and could give girls permission to waltz there.

usual froth.'

Heinemann's public relations department approached her that autumn about a proposal by Robert Pitman of the *Sunday Express* for a feature article on her to coincide with the publication of *Venetia*. They got a firm reply: 'Sorry! Nothing doing. Even if I wanted to oblige that particular section of the press, which I don't, I couldn't possibly be "interviewed". For years now I have consistently refused to see reporters, and to make an exception would not only be invidious, but would lead to trouble . . . If the *Sunday Express* wants to write about me, let it supply someone to write about my books, not about me – myself.'

As always, *Venetia* sold its 60,000 copies without help from the *Sunday Express*. It is indeed a love story, but Georgette Heyer was wrong to think it was without humour. It opens with an entrancing, characteristic, bit of dialogue:

'A fox got in amongst the hens last night, and ravished our best layer,' remarked Miss Lanyon. 'A great-grandmother, too! You'd think he would be ashamed!' Receiving no answer, she continued, in an altered voice: 'Indeed you would! It is a great deal too bad. What is to be done?'

His attention caught, her companion raised his eyes from the book which lay open beside him on the table and directed them upon her in a look of aloof enquiry. 'What's that? Did you say something to me, Venetia?'

'Yes, love,' responded his sister cheerfully, 'but it wasn't of the least consequence, and in any event I answered for you. You would be astonished, I daresay, if you knew what interesting conversations I enjoy with myself.'

'I was reading . . .'

'. . . What is it?' she returned, glancing at the volume. 'Ah, Greek! Some improving tale, I don't doubt.'

'The Medea,' he said repressively. 'Porson's edition, which Mr Appersett lent to me.'

'*I* know! She was the delightful creature who cut up her brother, and cast the pieces in her papa's way, wasn't she? I daresay perfectly amiable when one came to know her.'

Having thus both caught our attention and told us a remarkable amount about her heroine and her situation, Georgette Heyer has time to paint it in greater depth before she introduces her to the classic Mark I hero, swashbuckling arrogance, cynically bored eyes and all. He finds Venetia blackberrying on his estate, mistakes her for a country wench, calls her 'beauty's self' and promptly kisses her. She has known at once that he must be the local bad baron, and turns on him capping his quotation. 'I'm Damerel, you know,' he tells her:

'Yes, so I supposed, at the outset of our delightful acquaintance. Later, of course, I was sure of it.'

'Oh, oh – ! "My reputation, Iago, my reputation!"' he exclaimed, laughing again. 'Fair Fatality, you are the most unusual female I have encountered in all my thirty-eight years!'

'You can't think how deeply flattered I am!' she assured him. 'I daresay my head would be quite turned if I didn't suspect that amongst so many a dozen or so may have slipped from your memory.'

'More like a hundred! Am I never to learn your name? I shall, you know, whether you tell me or not.'

'Without the least difficulty! I am very much better known in this country than you, for I'm a Lanyon of Undershaw!'

Pride has met pride, and humour, humour, and they are launched on a volley of quotation and cross-quotation in which Georgette Heyer makes up for her past abstemiousness. She had been re-reading Shakespeare's plays, Restoration drama and related works, including Aubrey's *Lives*, and had written sadly to Frere that she found she could not have Damerel quote him: his *Lives* of Kenelm and Venetia Digby had not yet appeared in print in 1818, when *Venetia* is set. 'You may think this frivolous of me, but have you ever *read* what Aubrey said of Venetia? "A beautiful, desirable creature." Also, "about the eyelids great sweetness." Well, you see what I *mean*? Ben Jonson has one or two nice phrases, and I think I may find something in Aurelian Townsend, and Habingdon, both of whom wrote poems to her. My hero, I should add, is rather given to quotation.'

Luckily for her, it turned out that Aubrey's *Lives* had been published in 1813, so Damerel had his quotations after all. The book is thick with them, used like the Regency language as a kind of distancing for the serious romantic plot. You could almost say of the best of Georgette Heyer's romances that they are, like poetry, about emotion recollected in tranquillity, or seen from a distance. As well as the quotations, this book has another unusual element. There is a good deal of natural description, used consciously to convey romantic mood. Venetia, having begun to fall in love with Damerel, wakes up next morning:

A new day, fresh with new promise, set her tingling: the

thrush's trill became a lure and a command; she slid from the smothering softness of her feather-bed, and went with a swift, springing step to the window, sweeping back the blinds, and thrusting open the casement.

A cock pheasant, pacing across the lawn, froze into an instant's immobility, his head high on the end of his shimmering neck, and then, as though he knew himself safe for yet a few weeks, resumed his stately progress. The autumn mist was lifting from the hollows; heavy dew sparkled on the grass; and, above, the sky was hazy with lingering vapour. There was a chill in the air which made the flesh shudder even in the sun's warmth, but it was going to be another hot day, with no hint of rain, and not enough wind to bring the turning leaves fluttering down from the trees.

Had Georgette Heyer perhaps been re-reading *Persuasion*, another book with a strong flavour of autumn in the countryside? Venetia herself is almost a carbon contrast to quiet Anne Elliot who let her family send away the man she loved. When Venetia's uncle intervenes and takes her to London and 'the loveliest autumn within her memory' begins to slide into winter, she fights for her happiness and returns to find Damerel drunk, the Mark 1 hero at his worst:

He was alone, sprawling in the carved armchair at the head of the table . . . He was always rather careless of his appearance, but never had Venetia seen him so untidy. He had loosened his neckcloth, and his waistcoat hung open, and his black hair looked as if he had been in a high wind . . . The harsh lines of his face seemed to be accentuated, and his sneer was strongly marked. As Venetia moved softly forward into the candlelight he at last turned his eyes and looked at her. She stood still, shyness and mischief in her smile, and a hint of enquiry. He stared uncomprehendingly at her, and then, startling her, lifted his hand to his eyes, to shut her from his sight, ejaculating in a thickened voice of repulsion: 'Oh God! *No!*'

Jane Eyre would have turned and fled, but Venetia stands her ground: 'Oh, Damerel, must you be foxed just at this moment? How *odious* you are, my dear friend!'

She is one of the most liberated of Georgette Heyer's heroines, and a great realist about men, having learnt about them from her brothers. A conversation with Lady Denny, early in the book, has established the double standard that obtains in Georgette Heyer's private world. Lady Denny, talking about men's encounters with what she calls 'the muslin company', concludes that these 'don't change their *true* affection in the least'. Now, Venetia, telling Damerel that she would build a willow cabin at his gate except that 'November is *not* the month for willow cabins', does not want him to promise a faithfulness he may not be able to achieve. If he must go on having orgies, 'I can always retire to bed, can't I?'

Having thus squared Damerel she turns to her intervening uncle and offers him the cup of tea his nervous stomach longs for. She has learnt what Frances did in *Pastel*, that 'men run the show and we just run the men'. It is not precisely the behaviour of a liberated female, but it works.

Chapter 7

*R*onald Rougier became a QC in April 1959 and his wife wrote: 'Ronald's frolic takes place tomorrow, and I think he'll be glad when it's over. *I* shall enjoy it hugely, but, then, *I* haven't got to walk around in fancy-dress.' There must have been a warm satisfaction for them both in this prosperous culmination of the career so bravely embarked on some twenty-five years before.

Georgette Heyer was working on *The Unknown Ajax*: 'I rather like him myself. He's a new one, too, which makes an epoch!' She took the almost finished typescript to Deal for 'the usual Bench and Bar Tournament', meaning to finish it in longhand, but had been '. . . in a very odd state when I left town, and I did nothing but sleep for several days! . . . Great display of tact and restraint on the part of G. R. Rougier, QC, who made no attempt to persuade me to leave Ajax behind, but managed to think up grand reasons why I shouldn't do a stroke of work!' Ronald was indeed the ideal supportive husband.

He supported her, too, when she received a letter from John Smith, who had taken over at Christy & Moore when Moore died the year before:

We have taken advice regarding the question as to whether you are liable to continue to pay commission to us in relation to those books which we negotiated on your behalf and our information is – and on reasonable authority – that you are. I have considered the matter personally very carefully and we

Ronald Rougier, QC. A devoted and supportive husband for almost fifty years, he was always her first reader.

have decided not to instigate any proceedings since these would be inevitably prolonged and unpleasant; we are frankly not concerned with the financial issues involved and have pursued the matter purely on principle. In the event of our winning an action of such nature we should, of course, not have wished to retain further commission and would have passed it to charity.

Alas, we seem sadly to have declined from those happy days when an Englishman's word was supposed to be his bond. The phrase is a cliché, and undoubtedly outmoded in an age when apparently even a contract is not.

Ronald called this letter a damned insult. Georgette Heyer wondered why Smith meant to give the commission to charity if he managed to collect it. As for her, Moore's slackness in his old age had plunged her literary affairs into a state of muddle from which they never entirely recovered, and she must have felt justified in refusing to go on paying commission to his firm on the books for which they had negotiated the contracts. John Smith, who liked and admired Georgette Heyer, wisely decided not to embark on what would have been an extremely painful process of law, dragging the woman who loved her privacy through the courts. The Rougiers were always meticulous in their financial affairs. This apparent exception shows how grave the provocation had been.

Writing to Frere about it, Georgette Heyer turned to a more cheerful subject. *The Unknown Ajax* was going well. 'Sithee, love, (as my new hero would say) it's noan so bad!' She had found a new language in the broad Yorkshire with which her hero chooses to tease his snobbish family. Hugo Darracott is one of her huge men like John Staple, very much the opposite of the Mark 1 hero. His grandfather and his Cousin Vincent both have harsh faces with deep, almost sneering lines, but Hugo, introduced to us and his family for the first time, is something quite different:

The Darracotts were a tall race, but the man who stood on the threshold dwarfed them all. He stood six foot four in his stockinged feet, and he was built on noble lines, with great shoulders, a deep barrel of a chest, and powerful thighs. He was much fairer than his cousins, with tightly curling brown hair, cut rather shorter than was fashionable, and a ruddy complexion. His nose had no aquiline trend: it was rather indeterminate; and this, with his curly locks and his well-opened and childishly blue eyes, gave him an air of innocence at variance with his firm-lipped mouth and decided chin. He looked to be amiable; he was certainly bashful, but for this there was every excuse. He had been ushered into a room occupied by five gentlemen attired in raiment commonly worn only at Court, or at Almack's Rooms, and he was himself wearing leathers and topboots, and a serviceable riding-coat, all of which were splashed with mud.

Since he is the child of a misalliance, his snobbish family jump to all the wrong conclusions about him. Recognizing this, he falls back into the broad Yorkshire of his childhood; shamelessly misleading them about his background. They know he was a major in the 95th, Harry Smith's regiment, but when he describes the discomforts of life in a mud hut, or even in prison, they think he is talking of his seamy youth, not his wartime experiences. Bland and blue-eyed, he fools them every time, telling his Cousin Anthea (who has been instructed to marry him and teach him manners by their fierce old grandfather) that he is engaged to a Yorkshire lass called Amelia Melkinthorpe. He tells Anthea and his grandfather (a tyrant like the one in *Penhallow*) that he has money, but in a tone that leads them to think he is boasting of some small sum.

Since the Darracott estate, again like the Penhallows' Trevellin, is mortgaged to the hilt, with land and buildings alike showing signs of improvidence and neglect, money is important. Anthea's delightfully practical mother sums it up: 'It is a great piece of nonsense to pretend that life is not very much more comfortable when one can command its elegancies.' Having been forced to spend the long years of her widowhood bringing up her two children in the discomfort of Darracott Place, watching her father-in-law spoil and bully her son Richmond, she longs to have Anthea marry Hugo, whose essential kindness she recognizes at once.

Money is a vital element in Georgette Heyer's world, but it must go hand in hand with what she would call 'quality'. The Darracott servants recognize quality in Hugo at once: his manners and his boots are good, and his linen impeccable; his coat was made by Scott. It is the family who go so far astray, from the moment when his Cousin Vincent christens him 'the lubber Ajax', quoting Shakespeare's *Troilus and Cressida*. This is another book, like *Venetia*, where Georgette Heyer allowed herself a volley of quotations, obviously aware that she had her audience totally in hand, and would be forgiven the highbrow indulgence.

It is interesting that she should choose to weave a thread from one of Shakespeare's more unpleasant plays into her tightly knit comedy of misunderstandings. She had quoted another of them, *Measure for Measure*, as prelude to *Penhallow*. It is a reminder that comedy is not necessarily written out of a happy heart. Georgette Heyer made no secret of her dislike of the world she lived in: 'Christ, why did I have to be born into this *filthy* age!' She created her private world, perhaps, because she needed something nearer to her heart's desire, and just because of this it provides an escape for her readers too. Interestingly enough, the set-up of *The Unknown Ajax* is very similar indeed to that of *Penhallow*, with an old tyrant of a grandfather letting his estate go to rack and ruin and spoiling the lives of his relatives. But where *Penhallow* is as near to tragedy as Georgette Heyer ever got, *Ajax* is golden comedy throughout. The difference lies in Hugo, who sweeps into the book, like a great gale of fresh air, with his irresistible healing sense of humour, and his gift of love. He can even deal with jealous Vincent and will use his Yorkshire brass to put the estate in order. And when it turns out that young Richmond has embroiled himself with the local smugglers, it is Hugo's cool head that saves the day, in one of Georgette Heyer's scenes of crisis piled on crisis that keep the reader hooked into the small hours.

And all the time the romantic action is salted with comedy. When the crisis is past, Anthea turns to Hugo: '"I can't believe that it wasn't a nightmare!" she said, walking straight into his arms, and hugging as much of him as she could.' There is nothing saccharine about this happy ending. Rachel Trickett, talking to the Jane Austen Society, spoke once of her laughter as healing like sunshine, and Norman Cameron described this vital element in two lines: 'Laughter, like sunlight in the cucumber, /The innermost resource that does not fail.' We all need it, and Georgette Heyer provides it in full measure.

She needed all her resources in 1959. The intense fatigue she had felt in the spring had been a warning sign, and she went into hospital in the autumn for what proved to be a minor operation for the removal of a benign tumour, writing cheerfully to Frere when she came out that no major operation lay ahead of her, although her digestive trouble might continue for a while and she would need further X-rays. It does not sound entirely hopeful news.

It was at this time that Frere apologized for having nagged her about John of Lancaster. In a December letter he was 'sorry you are feeling neglected with a capital N [about *The Unknown Ajax*], but I cannot think of any period during our long, chequered, and to me wholly delightful association in which you have not had every right to feel so.' *Ajax* was, in fact, selling even better than *Venetia* had, and by February of 1960 Georgette Heyer was describing her plans for *A Civil Contract*. 'If I do write it, it will be neither farcical nor adventurous, and will depend for success on whether I can make the hero as charming as *I* believe he was! And also, of course, if I can make a quiet story interesting. The period would be 1814–1815, and the culminating point the financial panic in London over Waterloo. I have always had a slight yen to do that – and to see Major Percy driving in a hired hack to Carlton House, with the two Eagles sticking out of the windows. I'll let you know definitely in a week or two.' In the meanwhile she had just '. . . perpetrated a 10,000 word job for a new Woman's magazine . . . for which Joyce [Weiner] demanded, and got, 500 gns. I think this nice work, don't you? I'd call it money for old rope, except that it cost me too much blood and sweat. The story is very old rope – badly frayed – an unblushing crib on the works of Georgette Heyer.'

There was not much time for convalescence. She was distracted by worry about her mother, writing an old friend in March 1960

that: 'I can't think of what we've been through without a shudder.'
Mrs Heyer had had bronchitis in December, with two nurses in
attendance, but though still very frail, and eighty-four, insisted on
making her own living arrangements. When they went wrong her
daughter and sons had to cope as best they might, and her
daughter was the one on the spot. Both her brothers were married,
but neither of them lived in London. The strain of all this made
her ill, she wrote, and 'Nor is my dear husband's attitude helpful.'
She reported Richard's comment: 'On the subject of Granny,
Father is manic, ducky, *so don't worry!*' He had added thoughtfully,
'And you can't really blame him.' Mrs Heyer's surviving son Frank
remembers her strong character and robust sense of humour with
affection, but she was suffering from an irreversible disease, old
age, which does not necessarily bring out the best in one, and her
immediate family were bearing the burden.

Richard was now 'known to bridge columnists as "one of our
younger Masters"!' His immensely proud mother wrote a friend
that she had spent 'the better part of three week-ends watching
him play in three major events'. But he had also 'informed me
that he has no immediate intention of entering the married state,
and as he is 28 I begin to despair'. After a lively description of
some of his current girl friends, she ended on a domestic note: 'I
must stop: there is a Chicken Arosa to be dealt with, and HAVE
Harrods remembered to send the Saffron?'

With all this going on, it became obvious that *A Civil Contract*
would not be finished in time for autumn publication. This
would mean a gap in the regular programme of a Heyer a year
to which the fans looked forward. As a substitute, Joyce Weiner
suggested a collection of short stories, and this duly appeared as
Pistols for Two that autumn. It contained 'A Clandestine Affair',
the story its author had described as 'an unblushing crib on the
works of Georgette Heyer'. It is indeed a reworking of the theme
of *Bath Tangle*, with Ivo, Marquis of Rotherham, appearing as
Lord Iver, and Lady Serena metamorphosed into Miss Tresilian.
She has jilted Iver just as Lady Serena did Ivo in *Bath Tangle*, and
the ending is predictable, though inevitably entertaining.

The fifth Lady Jersey, one of the patronesses of Almack's. She 'was known, in certain circles, as Silence; but anyone who supposed that her flow of light, inconsequent chatter betokened an empty head much mistook the matter'.
Frederica

There was not quite room in the short story for Georgette Heyer's inimitable blend of romance and humour, and if ever her work shows signs of the saccharine, it is in these. Love at first sight is all very well once in a way, but as hero after hero succumbs, one begins to miss her stabilizing irony. The four short stories she left out of the collection also show her covering the ground she knew best. Two of them, 'The Quarrel' and 'Incident on the Bath Road', were reworked as *April Lady* and *Cotillion* respectively, while the other two, 'Pursuit' and 'Runaway Match', are variations on the inexhaustible theme of the elopement.

They are all written with Heyer elegance, and show her, as always, totally at home with her background, whether it is the mechanics of duelling in the title story, or the details of travel on the Great North Road in 'A Clandestine Affair' and 'Hazard'. She had pages on the Great North Road in her notebooks and could do it, as she would have said, a treat. But the short stories really were written for the fans, and for money, with plenty of elopements, the girls all beautiful, and the men all nonpareils. There are saving touches of humour, of course, and 'Pistols for Two' itself is a touching and perceptive story of the jealousy between two boys, or very young men indeed. They learn at last that the beauty they have fought over has been engaged to the older nonpareil all along. 'This was shocking news. Each unsuccessful suitor tried to realize that his life was blighted, and failed.' Georgette Heyer's touch with the young male was perfect. The groups of idle, entertaining young men are one of the reliable background pleasures of her books, and laughter, like sunlight, has broken through again.

By January 1961 *A Civil Contract* was finished at last, and she was feeling the strain. 'I decided . . . I had ended it a trifle abruptly – as though I were bored stiff with it, which I was! – so I've slightly expanded the end.' She was going to parcel it up, and her kind friend Frere, who also lived at Albany, would take it to the office for her, as he had done the first draft. 'He may be feeling sick to death of the sight of it, but he can't be nearly as sick of it as I am!'

This was another bad winter. The three Rougiers had 'a riotous Christmas in Paris', but on returning she wrenched her back putting her heavy typewriter away on a bottom shelf. While she was still suffering from this she learnt that her brother Frank's wife was in hospital in Bath: 'She's an orphan, and was an only child, and her one surviving aunt was cruising in the Caribbean, so what *could* I do but go down to Bath for the weekend?' Meanwhile, an osteopath diagnosed her back trouble, and told her not to sit in easy chairs, or stoop, or climb stairs, this last particularly awkward as their chambers were up all those steps. 'Added to this, Mama had one of her thrombosic black-outs, and fell, cracking a rib; and I learnt that yet another literary pirate is cashing in on my work. So isn't life FUN?'

Once again, she had had a letter from a fan, telling her about yet another imitator, and including a list of the more obvious borrowings. It ended: 'A novelist such as Miss Heyer . . . is bound to have imitators but I would suggest that this particular book goes far beyond the line of what is permissible, and I wonder whether Miss Heyer is protected by Copyright from such plagiarists as this.' Georgette Heyer thought at first that the book was by the original offender, using a pseudonym. Sending the fan's letter on to Frere, she asked, 'Am I going to do anything about it? It makes me feel quite sick to know that another slug is crawling over my work.' But, 'I shouldn't think I have a hope of succeeding in any action.'

This was written before she had read the book. When she had, she drafted a careful letter to its publishers. 'I feel compelled to protest against the injustice done me by the author in omitting my name from her list of the works to which she declares herself to be indebted. It might well take the place of Jane Austen's, for while no one would suspect [the author] of owing anything to Jane Austen it must be obvious to many besides my unknown informant that she owes to me plot, incidents, character, several surnames, and such examples of Regency slang as she has used.' The last straw, she concluded, was when her fans accused her of 'publishing shoddy stuff under a pseudonym'.

The author began by denying the charge, and Georgette Heyer sat down to do a long and devastating analysis of her borrowings and historical howlers, including the confusing of the

*Gambling at Brooks's, one of the two leading men's clubs, by Rowlandson.
Captain Kendal, in* Sprig Muslin, *belonged to White's; Tory Adam, in* A
Civil Contract, *to Brooks's. Vast sums of money were lost at the gaming
tables of both.*

4th and 5th Lady Jersey, the wrong publication date for Walter
Scott's *Waverley*, and some verbal usages that could come only
from herself. A favourite phrase, 'to make a cake of oneself', she
had found in a privately printed memoir, unavailable to the
general public, and the spangles on the Prince Regent's coat
which made Brummell cut the connection (in *Regency Buck*) were
entirely her own invention. She got as far as getting counsel's
opinion, but went no further.

In the meantime she felt sick whenever she thought of it, and
her blood pressure was seriously up. But this, she thought, was 'far
more due to Richard's folly'. Her son Richard, the confirmed
bachelor, had lost his heart at last to Susanna Flint, estranged wife
of a fellow member of the British bridge team. Georgette Heyer's
first reaction was entirely predictable. 'Not so much square as
cubed', she was, simply, appalled when her son helped Susanna
leave her husband and set up her own establishment. It is one
thing to write about elopements, quite another to have the next
best thing happen in the family. No married heroine of hers had

ever left her husband for good, and, to complicate things still further, Susanna had two little boys. But like most of Georgette Heyer's stories, this one had a happy ending. When she and her future daughter-in-law met, it was friendship at first sight. Did she recognize Susie as one of her own golden girls? She might well have felt she had created her. Richard and Susie joined the Rougiers at Greywalls that summer and Susie 'never put a foot wrong'. A swift and friendly divorce made marriage possible next year, by which time Georgette Heyer had discovered, as a bonus, that she had acquired two delightful step-grandsons, of whom Susanna, the innocent party, had custody.

But at the time it was all a great shock, and cannot have been good for her health. 'What with one thing and another,' she summed it up, '1961 seems to me a Bake.' She went on writing angry letters to Frere about the new imitator, who had offended her profoundly. 'Fancy taking the Heyer-Hero No. 1 model, enigmatic, for your model, and producing a lifeless puppet! Why, there isn't a type that's Easier To Do!' And again, 'I want to get the taste of this horrid mess of a book out of my mouth. Tell them . . . to hurry up with my proofs! – *that* book may be middle-aged, but it isn't slipshod and its humour doesn't gruesomely fail to be funny!' In fact, she did admit to worry about *A Civil Contract*. She was 'for once in my life, anxious to see how it reads in print'. She hired a television set for the cricket season, probably as good an antidote to stress as any.

And the proofs of *A Civil Contract* must have cheered her. The book had profited from its longer than usual incubation and shows her plotting at the top of her form. It covers a longer space of time than most of her Regency romances and is dated with unusual precision. Beginning in January 1814 with Adam, the new Lord Lynton, summoned home from the Peninsular army to face bankruptcy, it ends, just as she had planned, with Waterloo and the financial panic it caused. A great deal happens in these seventeen months. Adam gives up his romantic love, Julia, to marry plain Jenny for her money. The most practical of all the Heyer heroines, Jenny marries Adam because she loves him, explaining to his sister Lydia on the wedding day that: '"He'll be comfortable: I'll see to that!" The intensity of her expression was broken by a wintry little smile. "You don't think that signifies, but it does. Men like to be comfortable."' More realist than her husband, who is still pining for beautiful Julia, she opens the bedroom door a crack as they drive away to start their honeymoon: 'You'll be wanting an heir, and I hope I shall give you one. I should like to have children, and the sooner the better. But that's for you to decide.' Her horrified husband tries in vain to think of 'something, anything, to say to her', and it is she, the plain, shy cit's daughter, who turns the conversation. 'This is a new thing for me, you know: to be going to stay in the country.'

The honeymoon does indeed contain '. . . awkward moments that were inevitable in the circumstances, but these had been overcome, thanks largely (Adam acknowledged) to the prosaic attitude adopted by his bride. If their union was devoid of romance, less embarrassment attached to it than he had foreseen. Jenny was sometimes shy, but never shrinking.' As she also swiftly learns how he likes his eggs and that he hates muffins and breakfast table conversation, he does indeed begin to find some comfort in what everyone has thought his disastrous marriage.

Julia, the romantic figure, behaves as badly as possible, but an equally serious problem is Jenny's doting father, who showers them with outrageous and embarrassing gifts. He is one of Georgette Heyer's best comic characters, a marvellous contrast to Adam's die-away widowed mother who can ruin her children's comfort with a phrase: '*Laughing*, my dear ones?' The book is about comfort, and money, and friendship, and many people think it Georgette Heyer's best. A lightly touched in romance between Adam's sister Lydia and his best friend Brough is at once a sop for the fans and a useful means of keeping the reader steadily aware of the time-clock ticking away through the short peace of 1814 to Napoleon's escape from Elba and the events leading up to Waterloo. Along with this theme goes that of

Lady Castlereagh, another formidable patroness of Almack's. She befriended Jenny in A Civil Contract.

Jenny's pregnancy, a difficult one made more so by the fact that she is in the hands of Dr Croft, a real figure, who was to be responsible for Princess Charlotte's death in childbirth in 1817. There is obviously no way Georgette Heyer can prophesy this. She pays her readers the compliment of assuming they will understand how disastrous his lowering diet is likely to be for Jenny. Adam and her father who have had one superlative row over the management of her pregnancy have another on the day she has her son, and by the time Adam restores his fortunes by buying shares instead of selling them, as his father-in-law advised, during the panic over Waterloo, the way is ready for them to become friends. Adam and Jenny have both learnt that there is more to life than dreams. They will 'have many years of quiet content: never reaching the heights, but living together in comfort and deepening friendship'. People who like *Emma* best of Jane Austen's books may well prefer this one among Georgette Heyer's.

In the later books, Georgette Heyer enjoyed weaving other themes in with the romantic one, and *A Civil Contract* is about an Englishman's love of his home. Its descriptions of Adam's town and country houses show her devotion to detail at its lively best. Jenny's rich father has arranged what is to prove an unpleasant surprise for her husband by furnishing their town house for them, and they return from their honeymoon to face the results:

> Mr Chawleigh had fallen a victim to the fashionable rage for the Egyptian and the classical styles. The Dowager had stripped the drawing-room of almost everything but the large Aubusson carpet, and on its delicately hued pattern were placed couches with crocodile-legs, occasional tables inlaid with marble and wreathed with foliated scrolls, lyre-backed chairs, footstools on lion-legs, and several candelabra on pedestals entwined with lotus and anthemion garlands.

Appalled by all this, Adam is recovering slowly when he is roused by 'the most spontaneous peal of laughter he had yet heard from Jenny':

> Mr Chawleigh, transforming the dressing-room into a bath-room, lined with mirrors and draped with silk curtains, had provided his daughter with a bath in the shape of a shell: a circumstance which prompted Adam to say, after a stunned moment: 'Clearly from Botticelli – the Birth of Venus!'

But he is impressed by the modern plumbing of the bathroom, and similarly Jenny, who has always thought boredom 'the

Richard and Susie's wedding. The Rougiers are on Richard's right. Georgette Heyer wrote that Susie was 'the daughter we never had, and thought we didn't want'.

inescapable lot of women', learns to love the country, discovering occupation there: 'In London one buys, but in the country one makes.' She will never have style, but she is a very much more useful lady of the manor than Adam's mother ever was, and there is a charming glimpse of her suckling the Honourable Giles and talking to Adam as she does so. She applies herself to agriculture because this is what interests him and becomes knowledgeable about 'sticklebacks from Boston Haven' and the farming innovations of Coke of Norfolk. It is a delicious, human, unromantic book and some of the fans were disappointed.

Chapter 8

𝒜 nother cause for anxiety in 1961 had been the state of affairs at Heinemann, where a takeover was threatened, and a palace revolution raging. The firm's future, and Frere's part in it, were both uncertain. When she received the contract for *The Nonesuch* from Frere in May 1962, Georgette Heyer asked to have the option clause that gave Heinemann first refusal of her next book deleted, reminding him that they had agreed back in 1947 that her contracts should never contain such a clause. Now, she said, she had belatedly noticed that the clause had slipped back into the contract for *Cotillion* and been there ever since. 'I admit my hackles rose when I read the Option-clause . . . But of course it's not *your* fault . . . It's not your business to be checking contracts: I freely own that it *is* mine . . . However great one's confidence in one's publishers may be one should not sign even their contracts without carefully reading them first.' There was certainly an unbusinesslike streak in the highly professional author, but the letter may have been written not so much to Frere as to Heinemann. She had a new contact there by June, and wrote to thank him for passing on a letter from a fan who wondered if she knew that Harry Smith of *The Spanish Bride* ultimately became Governor General of South Africa and named Ladysmith after his bride. 'Typical of Fans!' she wrote. 'Do I know that Smith was governor general of South Africa . . . ? "*NO*? You don't say!" seems to be the only answer.' This is the kind of patronizing assumption that infuriated her. She went on to say that *The*

Nonesuch had been 'written under difficulties, and I think it stinks. I had hoped to have finished it before my son's wedding tomorrow, but I can't manage it. Unless anything awful happens it'll be done by the end of next week.'

The wedding duly took place at Kensington Register Office, with a party at Albany afterwards. The Rougiers then went off as usual to Greywalls, and Georgette Heyer returned the galleys of *The Nonesuch* from there, wondering whether '"Tête à têtes" is right. Shouldn't both "têtes" be in the plural?' She went on to say that she was 'a bad proof-reader of my own work, but my husband will go through the page proofs for me'.

Richard and his new wife planned to join the Rougiers at Greywalls at the end of August, but the day before they were due an urgent telegram from Richard summoned Georgette Heyer to London. Her mother had had another very serious stroke. Richard, the only member of the family in town, had got her into hospital and stayed with her until she recovered consciousness, but the outlook was as bad as possible. Mrs Heyer was eighty-five, paralysed down one side and unable to speak. 'Life has been an ever worsening nightmare,' wrote her daughter to an old friend when it was over. Her mother had suffered 'every hateful circumstance she most dreaded, and had always hoped would never befall her . . . Only a monster could have wished her to linger on.'

It was the end of an era. Georgette Heyer herself was sixty now. It was thirty-seven years since her father had died that summer day just before her marriage, and though she had often been maddened by her mother, her mother had always been there. Her brothers were alive, Boris and his wife running the Lord Craven Arms in Northumberland, and Frank teaching at Downside, but neither of them had children. She was very much the head of the family that continued only in Richard. It was no wonder that she adored him, and a blessing that she now loved Susie too. Richard and Susie had been her loving support during this black time, as well as her mother's. When Richard came into the hospital room, she wrote, her mother's face lit up. And Susie had 'throughout done exactly what I've asked her to do'. She wrote in the same letter to an old friend that 'Richard's marriage is a huge success, and Our dear Susie the sweetest of daughters-in-law – far more like a daughter, in fact. Their behaviour throughout these appalling months has been – my brothers assert – beyond praise.' And she ended: 'I made a lot of Good Resolutions, when Richard married, about Never Intruding on them, or Making Demands, but Susie smashed the lot – so that I find myself wondering if all is well at 56 Cornwall Gardens, if I don't get a telephone call from her. She and Richard drift in and out, nearly always dining with us at least once a week, so that although it was an awful wrench, losing him, we soon got over it – and no longer listen for his key in the lock.'

She had lost one of her resident male readers, but she had gained a daughter. Susie made no secret of the fact that she did not read her mother-in-law's books, but then Georgette Heyer, who rather despised people who liked her books, did not discuss them even with Mrs Frere, who loved them. There was much else to talk about in the daily telephone calls, and Susie remembers her mother-in-law saying that she really knew more about Richard's life now he was married than she had before.

Through all that autumn's trauma of hospital visiting, Georgette Heyer remained the complete professional. She had asked to see page proofs as well as galleys of *The Nonesuch*, and found and apologized for some errors of her own. 'I had given the same name to Mrs Underhill's housekeeper and Sir Waldo's valet . . . I must be in my dotage . . . When you reprint, there's an error on page 294 – Not "scolded like a cat-purse", but "like a cut-purse". I wish I could correct my own proofs as well as I correct *other* persons' works! I went through the proofs of Carola Oman's new book and don't seem to have missed a thing.' The two friends habitually read each other's proofs and Georgette Heyer had even compiled the index for Carola Oman's *Britain against Napoleon*, published in 1942.

The Nonesuch was published in the autumn of 1962 and does show signs of strain. Its story of the irruption of the nonesuch of

Richard Rougier, QC. Georgette Heyer enlivened her letters with descriptions of his prowess at the bar and the bridge table, and on the golf course.

the title into a quiet north-country society has a minimum of plot, with elegant hero and sensible heroine kept apart by one absurd misunderstanding after another, culminating in Ancilla's extraordinary conclusion that the group of children Waldo tells her he is responsible for are all his bastards. The laughter is a little harsh, too. Impatience has taken the place of irony: the silly young women are getting more tiresome, and the silly young men less convincing. And where *A Civil Contract* had some lively new language – 'We are no more alike than a dock and a daisy', or 'Leaping at it like a cock at a blackberry' – there is something excessive about the slang here – 'You were as thick as inkle-weavers with him, of course! What miff-maff you do talk!' New readers might well stop there. The curious phrase about inkle-weavers duly turns up under 'Friendship' in Georgette Heyer's vocabulary book, but as usual it is unattributed and unexplained. She found it somewhere, and collected it, and that was that. The *Shorter Oxford English Dictionary* is no help here, but Dr Johnson defines an inkle as 'A kind of narrow fillet; a tape'. The inkle-weavers must have been girls who worked and gossiped in one of the industrial revolution's satanic mills.

Gossip plays a considerable part in *The Nonesuch* and tends to take the place of action. It looks as if, from time to time, maybe when she was short of inspiration, Georgette Heyer re-read her Jane Austen, both novels and letters, and this time had come on the famous phrase about three or four families in a country village as the ideal subject. Like *A Civil Contract* this book is 'neither farcical nor adventurous', but unfortunately the human interest has failed a little too. Naturally there are good scenes and comic moments, but this time Georgette Heyer was right to be critical. *The Nonesuch* had been written under difficulties, and it showed. But it was a typical enough Heyer to get her a new publisher in the United States. She had said she would think again about Putnam after *Sprig Muslin*, now, five books later, she moved to Dutton.

She had also been making up her mind about Heinemann. She had not left when Frere did, but stayed on through the autumn publication of *The Nonesuch*, and agreed to lunch with her new editor, Derek Priestley, at the Connaught early in January 1963, to talk things over, suggesting that he wear 'a Distinguishing buttonhole – unless you know me by sight?' But a few days later a persuasive letter from him got one of her firm replies: 'My decision wasn't reached without a great deal of thought. In fact, to be asked to think any more about it almost makes me drum with my heels . . . A lot of very murky water has been flowing under the Heinemann bridge, and I don't like it . . . I will merely say that I'm sorry, but my mind is made up.' Like several other authors who had worked with Frere, she was leaving Heinemann for The Bodley Head, and Frere's friend Max Reinhardt.

Her personal relationship with her publisher had always been intensely important to her. Now, at sixty, she must work out a new one. She wrote to Reinhardt that January: 'So Frere thinks it a pleasure to deal with me, does he? He must have forgotten how broad a view I've always taken of his duties towards me. My own opinion is that all Inkies are hell, and ought to be incarcerated.' They planned a lunch at Scott's to discuss her new book, but she had to postpone it. The strain of her mother's last illness had told on her, and she had now caught 'a New Germ' which she could not shake off. 'It is *not* conducive to the writing of breezy romances.' But she could give him the title of her new book: '*False Colours*, and my assurance that I do *know* what it's going to be about!'

By April, she was writing: 'Dear Mr Reinhardt – No: on second thoughts I'll alter that to Dear Max, because now that we have entered into what I hope will prove an enduring association the sooner we abandon formality the better it will be for both of us. I was always very formal with Ralph Hodder-Williams, and just think what came of it! Well, probably you don't know, but we split brass rags.' The Bodley Head, like Heinemann, were planning production of *False Colours* while she was still working on it, and she wrote to approve the advance publicity, and the jacket design by the well-known artist, Barbosa, who had done her jackets at Heinemann for years: 'I like it very much, and think it stands out as an unmistakable Heyer-Novel.' She had done about 40,000 words and hoped to finish the book in June, though she had had to waste 'two noisome days and nights, at Harrogate, attending the Northern Optical Congress . . . My husband was appointed Chairman of the Optical Council two years ago, and consequently I get dragged, kicking and scratching, to these appalling functions.' She described them more fully to an old friend: 'All the banquets and congresses I can't get out of – plus a succession of Expensive Full Evening dresses, *with* pale gloves no use after the first wearing, none of which I have the *least* other use for.' There were social problems too: 'Few of the Optics come out of one's own social drawer. So I have to be very careful not to offend tender susceptibilities by failing to recognize Mrs Brown, Mrs Robinson, and Mrs Jones.'

When she could, she said, she now got Susie to stand in for her on these occasions. She went on to describe the delights of having a daughter: 'All I ever have to do is to introduce Our Susie, and stand back smugly, awaiting the inevitable sequel of: "My dear, what a *sweeet* girl! I *do* congratulate you!" . . . Susie wins all hearts – including ours! Indeed we wonder what on earth we did *without* Our Susie! She is the daughter we never had, and thought we didn't want.'

It is characteristic of Georgette Heyer that though she would not appear in public on her own behalf, she did so, if sometimes reluctantly, on her husband's. This was part of her job as his wife. But then she had always immensely enjoyed his legal connection and liked his legal friends. One of the few mementoes she saved was the Programme of a Grand Day at Lincoln's Inn at which she was guest of honour. It was filed with her father's Programme for the National Peace Celebrations in 1919, and a note on a hearing of a House of Commons Committee in 1959, in the course of which the chairman quoted *The Reluctant Widow* to Ronald.

They were going to Copenhagen before their annual holiday at Greywalls in 1963, and she worked on *False Colours* until the last minute, writing on 19 June that she had finished it the day before. 'I am feeling slightly peculiar today, for last night was my first in bed for 48 hours! In fact, I worked non-stop for 24 hours, and the wonder is that what I perpetrated isn't at all bad. Very odd! I found, yesterday, that my brain was perfectly clear and concentrated, and I felt fine, while working, but as soon as I got up to answer the telephone or to do anything else, I appeared to be divorced from myself and my surroundings, and was wholly unable to concentrate on anything! I am now going to relax in a big way.' She was pushing herself, at sixty, as hard as ever, but admitted that: 'Often, when pausing to think of *exactly* the right word, I abandoned the task, telling myself to *get on!*' She had finished *Friday's Child* in just such a burst of energy, but had only been in her forties then.

By July she had received Bodley Head's first draft for the *False Colours* blurb, which got short shrift. 'For Christ's sweet sake – *NO!* My plots are abysmal, and I think of them with blood and tears; I did not say that I was especially fond of *False Colours*! What I may well have said was that I don't think it stinks as much as *The Nonesuch*. It is *not* my favourite – *The Unknown Ajax* and *Venetia* are the best of my later works. My style is really a mixture of Johnson and Austen – what I rely on is a certain gift for the farcical. Talk about my humour if you must talk about me at all! . . . I don't know about my historical *feeling*: I'd prefer a timely word about my exact detail! . . . I did warn you that I was hell-to-deal-with, didn't I? . . .' Finally, she suggested that Bodley Head '. . . talk about its being just the job for people who are fed-up with kitchen sinks and perverts, and want a gay romance, *with* authentic period detail? I know it's useless to talk about technique in these degenerate days – but no less a technician than Noël Coward reads me because he says my technique is so good. I'm proud of that.'

The blurb was duly revised along the lines she suggested, and the remark about the kitchen sink was picked up by a number of reviewers when the book came out in September. Georgette Heyer always knew exactly what she was doing. She had been invited to her second Buckingham Palace Garden Party that summer. 'Ronald wouldn't let me refuse . . . but I think once is enough!' A devoted adherent of the House of Stuart, she had been enraged when the Queen called her son Charles. 'She stamped her foot,' Frere remembers, 'and her eyes flashed.' Tea at Buckingham Palace was not the kind of recognition she wanted. Her good friend Carola Oman had won a couple of literary prizes by now, in 1948 and 1953, for lives of Nelson and Sir John Moore, and Georgette Heyer would have been more than human if she had not made a quiet personal comparison. It was, of course, an argument for the unfinished historical book, but it remained in its lavender in these busy and harassed years.

The Rougiers went to Belford in Northumberland that autumn to meet Richard and Susie and her two little boys, aged seven and five, who adored their stepfather. Georgette Heyer described the happy family holiday to a friend: 'It was a huge success, and the few other visitors at the Blue Bell (an old and loved haunt of ours) failed dismally to unravel our relationships! It was really funny to watch their puzzled faces when the babies hailed Ronald as "Father"! He rather liked it – flattered, I think! As Richard and Susie call him Father, it must have seemed very odd to hear two infants calling him Father too! Dommy stuck to "Richard's Mummy", but Noël found this too much of a mouthful, and called me Mama!!!'

False Colours came out early in September when they were still at Belford. Georgette Heyer was delighted with the Barbosa jacket, and Susie with the dedication to her, and the book was already reprinting by the middle of the month. The challenge of her new publishers had elicited a new plot about twins, and a new twist to the marriage of convenience. Compelled to masquerade as his identical elder brother, the younger and more sober of the Fancot twins inevitably falls in love with his brother's new fiancée. Lively complications ensue, and there are some admirable comic scenes and characters, notably the twins' scatter-brained, entrancing mother, and her lifelong suitor, fat Sir Bonamy Ripple – 'one of my more felicitous creations', said his author. The heroine, Cressy, is one of Georgette Heyer's quiet, strong-minded young women who have been brought up mainly by their fathers. A robust realist about men, she easily routs the blackmailing mother of one of the elder Fancot's fancies in a splendid comic scene. Her relationship with Kit and with his absurd mother has the underlying vein of warm

Lake Placid, September 6, 1963

Dear Mrs. Heyer,

On behalf of hundreds of political women prisoners in Rumania, I wish to express their thanks and mine for having helped us escape — for a few hours at least — from the weary drabness of our prison days and the evil that surrounded us.

In 1948, a year before my arrest, I had read — and revelled in — FRIDAY'S CHILD, and as I have a very retentive memory I was able to tell it to my cell-mates, practically verbatim. At first it was very difficult, because I had to translate as I went along and didn't want them to lose one of the quips and Ferdy-isms which are so much part of it. With time I acquired skill and in this way Hero (Kitten), Sherry, Gil, Isabella became our close and much-loved friends who were often asked to visit us and received a warm welcome and aroused hearty – but hushed – laughter. Truly, your characters managed to awaken smiles, even when hearts were heavy, stomachs empty and the future dark indeed!

You probably don't know that life in a Rumanian political prison is particularly harsh. Political prisoners are strictly forbidden :

a) all communication with their families, lawyers,etc.
b) books, newspapers, magazines,
c) writing materials of any kind,
d) transistors,etc.

During the 12 years I spent in prison I didn't see a written page. My memory however, could not be sealed up and thanks to it and to you, my fellow-sufferers begged, again and again, to hear " What Kitten Did Next".

I decided then, if I ever came out of prison and from behind the Iron Curtain, to write and thank you most gratefully for this ' jewel of the past and present" and wish you to remember that although I am no longer there, your jewel is still helping those that carry on their weary load of prison years.

With warmest regards,

Sincerely,

[signature]

sgd. (Miss) Nora SAMUELLI

Mrs. Georgette HEYER
c/o G. PUTNAM's SONS
200 Madison Avenue
New York 16, N.Y.

Letter from a Romanian admirer. Most fan letters got short shrift, but Georgette Heyer treasured this one.

humanity of *Venetia, The Unknown Ajax* and *A Civil Contract*, but fatigue does show here and there. The name Fancot had been used in *April Lady*; Patience Askham and her loving, unworldly family are a straight repeat of Patience Chartley and hers in *The Nonesuch*, and when, at the end, Kit racks his brains for a way out of their imbroglio, one does rather feel that the author was doing so too during those forty-eight sleepless hours.

An obvious problem here was that her new contacts at The Bodley Head could not be expected to be deeply acquainted with her previous work. This is one book that would have benefited from a little editing, but when Max Reinhardt made a mild suggestion about a bit of its Regency language, he received a sharp set-down from his formidable new author. Totally co-operative in the normal way, she could be ferocious when roused. Bold young editors might be reduced to tears, and she herself had a phrase for it. 'I fixed him [or her],' she would say, 'with a basilisk stare.' No wonder she was handled, always, with kid gloves, and known, lovingly, among her friends, as 'The Duchess'.

She was firm about *Woman's Journal*, who must publish to suit Bodley Head, or not at all. The letter about the Belford holiday has a hopeful reference to a possible film of *False Colours* with Anna Neagle ('a fan of mine') playing Lady Denville and her husband Herbert Wilcox directing. There was talk, too, of an all-English all-star production of *An Infamous Army* for the anniversary of Waterloo, but nothing came of either of these promising ideas. Georgette Heyer's books with their brilliant plotting and distinctive style and language should be naturals for film or television, but not, perhaps, with their strong-minded author at the director's elbow.

The letter of thanks from the Romanian political prisoner who kept herself and her fellow prisoners sane by telling the story of *Friday's Child* over and over again reached Georgette Heyer that autumn, and she treasured it. The woman who wrote it was safe in the United States, and Georgette Heyer was able to thank her for the heart-warming tribute. She and Ronald made two new friends in 1963. Ronald sat next to Donald Sinden at the Garrick Club and they got talking about the House of Plantagenet, as Sinden was playing Richard Plantagenet in *Henry VI* at Stratford. Amazed at his new acquaintance's wealth of information, Sinden was surprised to learn that he was a barrister, not an historian. His wife was a Heyer fan and he presently asked Ronald to bring his famous wife to dinner. Ronald agreed, but stipulated that she would want to come simply as Mrs Rougier. But for once their family signals seem to have been crossed. It became obvious in the course of the evening that Mrs Rougier wrote, and John Gielgud, another of the guests, put the question to her directly. A quick exchange of glances followed, and Ronald explained.

The friendship throve and Georgette Heyer signed all Diana Sinden's copies of her books, if she did not discuss them. When Donald Sinden appeared in *London Assurance* in 1970 and it was decided to set the play back from 1840 to 1820 he asked Georgette Heyer if she would come and watch the preview for anachronisms. She demurred, 'I finish in 1818,' but came and pointed out that Donald Sinden ought not to be wearing his Hessians to a ball, and that the old-fashioned sixty-three-year-old he played would take steak and ale, not chocolate, for his breakfast.

There was good news from America in 1963. Georgette Heyer's new publisher, Dutton, reported successful sales of their first title, *The Nonesuch*, which was published that year and surprised and pleased its author by getting good coverage in middle and far western newspapers. She liked the longer, full style of American reviewing. When *False Colours* came out there in the spring of 1964 it achieved a long review in *Time Magazine* which Reinhardt described cautiously as 'splendid and, of course, like everything in that magnificent magazine, slightly inaccurate, but with excellent publicity for you.' The *Time* reviewer began with a quotation from *Venetia* to illustrate Georgette Heyer's use of slang and went on to say that the 'genteel reading cult that made her for years a runaway best-seller in England is now spreading to the US, proliferating vociferously at ladies' luncheons and lending libraries.' He spoke of the 'spell of a slight-prose master' and concluded: 'In an age of prurience and pornography, Georgette Heyer's main appeal is in the faultless re-creation of a world of manners and decorum.' She must have been pleased with this, despite the errors: 'I learn, with interest, that my stylish Albany apartment is stuffed with antiques and that I am married to a London lawyer named Richard Rougier. However, the rather repulsive article is eminently quotable, so I expect Dutton is pleased.' Dutton undoubtedly were. There were American fan clubs now, dressing up in Regency costume, talking in Regency language and exquisitely taking snuff in the manner of Beau Brummell.

Elliott Graham of Dutton, who visited her in Albany, described the occasion after her death. Her readers, he said, 'would have found her as admirable as they always imagined she must be. One might expect her to be a recluse, as fragile as the invalid Elizabeth Barrett in her Wimpole Street bedroom, or as shy as Emily Dickinson in her father's house in Amherst. Actually, she was a vigorous, athletic-looking woman with a clear skin, a shock of dark hair, a woman with an assured, no-nonsense manner, whose movements were quick, who dressed well in wool suits, who could knit quietly for hours or who could, if the occasion warranted it, talk endlessly in an entertaining manner. She was always a bright and amusing person to meet, and her conversation sparkled with wit.' He went on to describe the chambers: 'Done in various shades of brown and gold, with shelves of books covering entire walls, and with a striking full-length portrait of the author as a young woman hanging over the living-room fireplace.'

He had been interested, too, in what she said about women. She would have been happier in the Middle Ages, she told him. Women then actually had a great deal of independence because of the dowers they carried with them and the power they wielded, often for long periods of time, while their husbands were off fighting. The reign of Queen Victoria, on the other hand, had been a bad time for women because the Queen's overdependence on the Prince Consort set a fashion that undermined their position. It is an interesting comment from Georgette Heyer, who always let her husband seem to be the decision maker. But then, she was a remarkable example of the woman who successfully combines career and marriage. It might not have worked so well if she had yielded to the pressure of publishers and fans and gone public herself.

She was at work on *Frederica* by January 1964, but had to

cancel a lunch with Reinhardt because of a bad bout of flu. 'Too sickening, and just when I had meant to get down to *Frederica*, too. I am not one of those who work well – or at all – under adversity.' She had got over her resistance to being paperbacked, and Pan were issuing her Heinemann titles in chronological order. She had just seen the jackets of eight of their books: 'Two quite attractive, one very good, some poor, and one – *The Infamous Army* – ghastly! This depicts the battlefield, with glamorous Female, dressed in a yellow silk pelisse, and a modern hair-do, supporting a wounded soldier.' His uniform was all wrong, 'And what the hell was the Lady Barbara doing on the battlefield, anyway? A nasty, cheap job!' But Pan promised to let her see roughs of her future jackets and she was pleased when Penguin, who had published *Devil's Cub* in 1953, made an offer for *False Colours*, though she scrupulously asked Reinhardt if they were not in honour bound to offer it to the New English Library, who, she felt, had been given a hard time by Heinemann when they had previously been angling for her.

A request from Reinhardt for the Heinemann sales figures for *The Nonesuch* to compare with those for *False Colours* revealed a gap in her accounting system. Her latest figures from Heinemann were with her accountant and she had given up taking copies before passing them on. With over thirty titles in print and to be accounted for, this is hardly surprising, but it does suggest a persisting dangerous element of muddle, with no one in overall control of either the publishing or the financial side of her ramifying literary affairs. From time to time a wry remark in a letter shows her grappling with paperwork that might well have been spared her.

But for the moment she and Reinhardt agreed with satisfaction that *False Colours* was notably out-selling *The Nonesuch*. They had reached a comfortable understanding as correspondents, with Georgette Heyer saying 'don't interrupt', as she had, before, to Louisa Callender, or pointing out that 'Meticulous Civility to my Publisher is my watchword'. When Reinhardt signed himself 'Your humble servant' she capped it

A card party, by Cruikshank. Horry, in A Convenient Marriage, *played her disguised husband for a lock of hair, while the brooch Lady Denville lost at cards caused all the trouble in* False Colours.

with a mediaeval phrase, 'Wishing you long life and well-enduring'.

She had met and made friends with Max Reinhardt's American-born wife by now. Mrs Reinhardt remembers being nervous before her first meeting with her husband's formidable new star author, whose books she and her friends had loved at school in America. But when they dined with the Rougiers in Albany she found nothing formidable about Georgette Heyer as a hostess, and was aware of the vein of shyness beneath the forceful personality. Georgette Heyer had never let herself be lionized and therefore had never developed into a lion. She really did not seem to understand what a celebrity she was. And she and Ronald were the best of hosts, serving a delicious meal without help. It was the first of many such dinners, the kind of entertaining the Rougiers liked, with sometimes the Freres and sometimes Richard and Susie to make the party up to six. Georgette Heyer did all the cooking herself, from the best ingredients, including caviar, from Fortnum & Mason: Ronald looked after the excellent wine and changed the plates. They were friendly evenings, with general talk, steering clear of too controversial political issues out of deference to Ronald's diehard conservatism, still more entrenched than his wife's. And when the talk turned to Georgette Heyer's work, she deferred to Ronald, letting his be the last word, though the basic decision may have been hers. There were occasional bursts of laughter at her expense, too, when she indulged in one of her vehement anti-American speeches, then remembered Mrs Reinhardt's American birth and hastened to apologize.

Reinhardt asked for the usual advance outline of *Frederica* in February and she grumbled at first: 'Why on earth the Trade should Want to Know what This Book is about I cannot imagine, for the dim-wits ought to know by now that my books aren't About anything; and also that all my faithful public wants to know is that it is the Regency mixture as before.' But *Frederica* was 'coming into shape fast, now that I'm better acquainted with the Merriville family – not to mention their embarrassing dog. I suppose you don't happen to know how a schoolboy could contrive to get himself unbeknownst into a balloon? No: well, Ronald says he couldn't conceal himself amongst the sandbags, but I do Want little Felix to be carried off in a balloon . . .' She duly and characteristically provided the outline:

Where was I? Oh, yes! DRIP FOR THE TRADE! Here you are! This book, written in Miss Heyer's lightest vein, is the story of the adventures in Regency London of the Merriville family: Frederica, riding the whirlwind and directing the storm; Harry, rusticated from Oxford, and embarking with enthusiasm on the more perilous amusements pursued by young gentlemen of ton; the divine Charis, too tenderhearted to discourage the advances of her numerous suitors; Jessamy, destined for the Church, and wavering, in adolescent style, between excessive virtue and a natural exuberance of spirits; and Felix, a schoolboy with a passion for scientific experiment. In *Frederica*, Miss Heyer has created one of her most engaging heroines; and in the Marquis of Alverstoke, a bored cynic who becomes involved in all the imbroglios of a lively family, a hero whose sense of humour makes him an excellent foil for Frederica.

Reinhardt wrote gratefully: 'The blurb is fine and you realize of course that with these two paragraphs of yours alone we have already booked orders for several thousand copies of *Frederica*.' Inevitably, this meant pressure on Georgette Heyer to finish the book in time for autumn publication, and the vital date of the last sailing to catch the Christmas market in Australia and New Zealand. It seems strange that it should have occurred to no one that the willing scribe might take a year off so that her books could be promoted, like most authors', after they had been finished and handed in. But she would probably have been the first to reject such a suggestion. She was always her own hardest taskmaster and may even have preferred this high pressure method of production which made it possible to treat the books as mere light-hearted nonsense, in contrast to the serious mediaeval work that still lay, neglected, in the Albany chambers.

In March she wrote that *Frederica* was progressing slowly. 'I am getting to know the people in it, and have just introduced a pleasing hound, who will probably harry the cows in the Green Park. The youngest member of Frederica's family is mad about steam-locomotion, and coal-gas. Why I do these things I can't imagine, for as I don't know anything about such matters it means Work; and I am for ever consulting various volumes, borrowed from the London Library.' She was obviously feeling better and was planning a party in April, but a visit from Barbosa to discuss the jacket for *Frederica* proved untimely: 'Being worried at this stage about jackets is something "up with which I will not put".' She ended with a familiar cry: 'I've written about 20,000 words, and I think they stink.'

Woman's Journal discovered that *Frederica* would be the twenty-first Heyer novel they had serialized and asked for an interview to mark the occasion. She refused to make an exception to her long rule, but agreed to be photographed; 'seated at my desk, so to speak. Wholly repellent, but they'd probably like the idea.' Reinhardt enthusiastically recommended a photographer, but Georgette Heyer then jibbed. 'I am not what is known as a Good Subject, and generally look like a cross between a horse and the late Lady Oxford.' In the end, Reinhardt and Frere put their heads together and Frere approached her about finding an earlier photograph: 'Of all the low, cunning snakes! So you had the happy idea of sicking Frere on to me, did you?' She had found 'the last one ever done of me – in 1946, if the legend on the back is to be believed . . . Large tears are only with difficulty prevented from dropping on this page: I did *once* look like that! – I promise you I did! "*Eheu fugaces, Posthume, Posthume*"! I now propose to dwindle into a decline – a resolution only strengthened by a glance at my current novel. "Old, old, Master Shallow!"' And a postscript. 'The combination of the photograph and *Frederica* has convinced me that I ought to have been put down *years* ago.'

The Rougiers went to Scotland for Whitsun, but she caught a 'cataclysmic cold' and progress with *Frederica* continued slow. She warned Reinhardt that she thought it was going to be long and was afraid it might not be finished by the end of June. But she had been through what she had done so far and been 'a *little* cheered', and *Woman's Journal* were being obliging about the possible delay. She was looking forward to the authors' ball to which Reinhardt had invited them. The Freres would be there too. 'Perhaps the sight of *both* my Favourite Publishers will act as a tonic and an inspiration!'

She enjoyed the authors' ball. 'In different company I should

Harding and Howell, Drapers, 89 Pall Mall, 1810. Frederica's sister Charis made her own ball dress from material bought in a shop like this, and a sketch in the Ladies' Magazine.

have hated it; as it was, I found it very cosy!' This sums up her attitude to such occasions. Always a better host than guest, she liked her own parties best but would make an effective entrance to those of her own publishers. Frere remembers a garden party at the Windmill Press in the Forties when she turned up in full rig and huge hat only to be introduced by a nervous publicity man as Enid Bagnold. She thought this enormously funny and never let him forget it. On that occasion they had arrived in their own recently purchased Rolls-Royce. Ronald had a taste for large and expensive cars.

Frederica was still unfinished when Georgette Heyer was taken ill at the end of June and admitted to the private wing of Guy's Hospital for the removal of a kidney stone. 'It was far from funny,' she wrote, adding that she had an immense scar and the doctors had warned her that she would be 'an invalid for about 6 weeks, and not really-and-truly at the top of my form again

until Christmas'. They were going to Greywalls for her convalescence, and, 'I shall take *Frederica* north, and might even do
some work on her!' In the meanwhile she was reading Dickens,
'a sure sign of old age!' But he had always been a favourite of
hers. She found Scott (a favourite of Ronald's) heavy, and
Trollope superficial. She was a great admirer of craftsmanship.
Among modern authors she read Agatha Christie as well as Ivy
Compton-Burnett; Alastair Maclean and Noël Coward;
Compton Mackenzie and her friend Christopher Landon; and
also Angela Thirkell, another creator of a private world, but one
where the snobbery got out of hand. At the theatre, she was more
interested in the players than the play. Most understandably, she
had no patience with either Desdemona or Anna Karenina, or,
indeed, for Russian gloom in general. If she had been one of
Chekhov's three sisters they would have got to Moscow. In
music, she and Ronald enjoyed Wagner together, but it was
Bach she played on the gramophone when she was writing, both
perhaps understandable choices in one who was tone deaf.

The doctors had been over-optimistic. By October they
admitted it might be a year before she was fully herself again.
And she was suffering from repercussions, 'including a dropped
metatarsal arch, which is hell'. Added to this they had the
decorators in, and life was 'like the Mad Hatter's Tea Party' as
they moved from room to room. It seems extraordinary to have
the decorators in at such a time, but this was doubtless the kind
of decision she had always taken and it occurred to neither of
them to alter it. It was hardly surprising that there was no news
of *Frederica*, though Ronald 'would tell you – impressively – that
I was playing a lot of Patience. The Family regard this as a sign
that I am revolving Plans for a Book . . . I begin to see my way.
Unfortunately, plans for the next, and *much* more amusing book,
insist on obtruding, and have to be repressed.'

The Bodley Head had re-scheduled *Frederica* for publication in
April or May of 1965 and with the workmen gone at last,
Georgette Heyer wrote in November that: 'I have resumed
work, a little painfully, on that ill-omened Frederica.' But

publication would have to be postponed until the autumn because of her commitment to *Woman's Journal*, and, besides, she was suffering from post-operative adhesions and still getting ferociously tired. A morning's shopping left her incapable of any 'real work' and she decided that it would be folly to try to finish *Frederica* for spring publication. 'I wish I weren't failing you like this . . . Never before have I fallen down on a contract. Try to forgive me! You can't feel more disappointed and furious than I do. Yes, and Miss Lindsay, of Harrods Book Dept., tells me that she is assailed by hundreds of customers, demanding to know *Why* no new Heyer, and *When* a new Heyer? One way and another, this has *not* been our lucky year.' Wishing Reinhardt and his wife a pleasant Christmas she wrote that: 'We are spending ours quietly – thank God! I detest the Festive season, when there are no children to make it worth while. We are going to Richard and Susie on Christmas Day . . . and they are dining-and-bridging with us on Boxing Day. And I shan't have to cook turkeys and hams, and plum puddings. Ha!'

By February she was working on the last two or three chapters of *Frederica*: 'I don't think the book is *much* more than twice as long as it should be.' She would send it as it stood to *Woman's Journal* and let them do their own cutting. 'But your copy, and Dutton's I shall mess about a bit, cutting out irrelevancies, and excess verbiage.' She was planning to retype the whole 145,000-odd words herself, cutting it as she went. Meanwhile a fan had written to the Queen suggesting that as Scotland 'pays honour to Sir Walter Scott' and Ayr to Burns with statues, 'Would it not be a kindly act to likewise show honour to Britain's most popular writer – Miss Georgette Heyer?' Thanking Reinhardt for sending her copies of the fan's letter and the Home Office's civil reply, Georgette Heyer said that she hoped he did not want the fan's letter back, 'because it has gone into my collection of Laughs!' This was not the kind of recognition she wanted. She preferred a review from *The Sacramento Bee* which said that: 'Of the modern English novelists, probably none has been so undervalued by critics, and so welcomed by readers as Georgette Heyer.'

Ronald Rougier's career continued to prosper. He had been made a Deputy Chairman of Essex Quarter Sessions in 1964, and by the spring of 1965 his wife was well enough to go and see him in action. She wrote a friend that she 'found him very impressive, and (as I told him) almost *respected* him!' Richard, too, was 'bidding fair to become one of our Busiest Juniors', and Georgette Heyer sympathized with her daughter-in-law when, like his father before him, he habitually rang up from miles away to say his case had been carried over and he would not be back that night.

They went to Rye for Ronald's Easter golf, to Sweden at Whitsun, and then in the summer to Ireland with Richard and his family. Georgette Heyer wrote a friend that she still got tired very quickly but was 'apparently lucky to be alive – if you call it lucky, in this disgusting era!' She was catching up on her social duties, and wrote to thank Reinhardt for 'a lovely party'. She liked parties where she knew people; it was only the cold-blooded publishers' circuit type of occasion that she avoided like the plague. She was firm about other things too. When Reinhardt asked her if she had seen *Frederica* on the *Evening Standard*'s Best Seller list, he got an uncompromising answer: 'No, sir, I did *not* see the *Evening Standard*. I will not allow a Beaverbrook paper across my threshold.'

Herbert Wilcox was in New York hoping to interest an American company in a TV series of her books beginning with *False Colours*, but she wrote cautiously: 'I've had so many large schemes of this sort put up to me that I'm punch-drunk, and set very little store by them.' She wrote on: 'The root of the matter is in him, for he insists on two points: that it must be done *well*, or not at all – and in colour, and that I must vet all period detail and dialogue, and mine must be the last word.' The terms were presumably too tough for the Americans, and nothing came of this promising project, but at least Dutton were making *Frederica* their top book for the season.

Georgette Heyer had been stung by a mosquito when they were in Sweden, and wrote in September that it had turned septic and still would not heal. 'My doctor has begun to talk about Skin Specialists and Skin Grafts. Not if I know it! I've twice been nearly killed by Skin Specialists.' Instead, she said, she spent her time on the sofa knitting. It must have made her family anxious. Her brother remembers that persons who wished their socks darned were reduced to challenging her by having a public go at it themselves. She would cook, lovingly, for her male dependants, and indeed put on a good deal of weight in her later years as a result, but other forms of domesticity were anathema to her.

The Bodley Head were planning an autumn launching party for *Frederica*, during which they would release fifty balloons from their roof garden, each one carrying a card entitling the finder to a free copy of the book, and Reinhardt hoped that Georgette Heyer would come, or at least give them a quote about the book. 'Absolutely NOT,' she replied. '. . . Only Felix saves it from utter boredom! . . . When I compare it to the three of the same genre, which I *do* think good, I could weep! *Essayons encore!*' And then, a characteristic postscript: 'I *did* warn you, didn't I? that I was Uncooperative. Frere once, just before the war, tried to get me to Lend Myself to a bit of publicity, and I was *most* co-operative. I offered to lunch with him at the Savoy, bringing with me my Irish wolfhound bitch – 32" at the shoulder! – and *assured* him that after we had been refused admittance to a leading London restaurant we should have acquired all the publicity we could want – even if no lunch! Somehow or other the suggestion found no favour with him.' The story had changed a little over the years, as stories will, but her stand remained the same.

When *Frederica* began to come out in *Woman's Journal* a reader pointed out a rare error. Researching Felix's beloved engineering works at the London Library, Georgette Heyer had been misled by a reference to an iron foundry in Soho and placed it in London instead of Birmingham. She minded this very much, but there was nothing to be done about it.

Presumably the three other books of the same genre that she preferred to *Frederica* were *Venetia*, *The Unknown Ajax*, and *A Civil*

Contract, which all have more character and human interest than adventure, but as usual she did her current book less than justice. It would, it is true, have profited from some judicious cutting, but it is a significant contribution to her world of manners and morals, an interesting development and advance on *Sylvester*. Like Sylvester, the bored and cynical Marquis of Alverstoke is becoming sick with pride when the irrepressible Merrivale[1] family burst into his life, and proceed to humanize him. 'You haven't snubbed *us*,' says Frederica significantly. Alverstoke is farther gone than Sylvester was, because he has also been corrupted just a little by the 'barques of frailty' with whom he has associated, and tends to look down on all women. Georgette Heyer was getting franker about this aspect of her heroes' lives. The plot is full of echoes of previous books, but some of the writing shows her at her ironic best:

> Lady Buxted's disposition was not a loving one. She was quite as selfish as her brother, and far less honest, for she neither acknowledged, nor, indeed, recognized her shortcomings. She had long since convinced herself that her life was one long sacrifice to her fatherless children; and, by the simple expedients of prefixing the names of her two sons and three daughters by doting epithets, speaking of them (though not invariably to them) in caressing accents, and informing the world at large that she had no thought or ambition that was not centred on her offspring, she contrived to figure, in the eyes of the uncritical majority, as a devoted parent.

How many readers would recognize this passage as Georgette Heyer's if they encountered it in a literary quiz? As for Felix, he is the triumph she thought him, and the book might well have been dedicated to Susie's little boys, Dominic and Noël, who had swept into her life as the Merrivale boys did into Alverstoke's.

1 The spelling of the name had changed since Georgette Heyer planned the book.

Significantly, Felix has the last word. Frederica and Alverstoke are engaged at last, and Alverstoke has undertaken the guardianship of her young brothers. 'Why shouldn't he wish to have us?' asks Felix, and goes on: 'Cousin Alverstoke, what I *particularly* wanted to ask you is, may I have a workshop at Alver? For experiments? If I promise *faithfully* not to blow the house up? If you *please*, Cousin Alverstoke?' *Woman's Journal* cut this, and Georgette Heyer was justifiably enraged.

A 'splendid row with Heinemann' that year cannot have been particularly good for her temper – or her blood pressure. Though they went on urging her to come back to them, her old publishers seemed to her not to be putting their heart into selling the titles they had, particularly their uniform edition. Worst of all, they had failed to do anything about *An Infamous Army* for the hundred and fiftieth anniversary of the Battle of Waterloo: 'Frere says they probably thought it was about a suburban station! But when I recall what a press it had, when it came out, and how it is recommended to cadets at Sandhurst, and to all schools, it makes me seethe with rage.' Her nephew, she said, when he was at Sandhurst 'couldn't restrain himself from piping up: "Please, sir, it's my aunt!!!" Or words to that effect.'

If Heinemann seemed lethargic, Bodley Head were being very active indeed, and *Frederica* surprised and pleased her by out-selling *False Colours* in the pre-Christmas sales. She had a characteristic wry comment: 'Some of *Frederica*'s success may be due to lack of competition: Carola Oman informs me that she can find no other Suitable Novel to give as a Christmas present.' They went to Edinburgh for Christmas and she promised Reinhardt that the New Year would be 'enlivened for you by news of my new book. At present I have none to give you, but don't worry! It always happens like this, but, somehow or other, the New Book *does* get written!'

Chapter 9

*T*he early months of 1966 were made hideous by a grave
new outbreak of financial trouble. Some basic misunderstanding had taken place between Georgette Heyer
and 'my *late* accountants . . . with the result that I now stand in
the pleasing position of owing the Company [her own company:
Heron Enterprises] something in the region of £20,000.' Serious
tax problems were involved, and she proposed to wind up Heron
Enterprises and asked that the contract for her new book, *Black
Sheep*, be made out for her personal signature.

It was an appalling crisis for a hard-working woman of sixty-
three to face. Luckily, she found a new accountant, Hale Crosse,
of Black Geoghegan & Till, who refused to be afraid of her, and
became a good adviser and friend over the years. But the sorting
out of the dangerous state of muddle into which the company
affairs had slid would take him some time. In the meanwhile, the
only good thing she could think of was 'the appearance on the
scene of Nicholas Rougier', her one grandson, born in February.
When Hale Crosse suggested that she sell Heron Enterprises
outright, her first reaction was that it was 'rather as if Susie were
offered X thousand pounds for Nicholas!'

What with one thing and another, she was suffering from a
mysterious virus that winter, and by March had still not made
much progress with *Black Sheep* and could not even provide an
advance outline. There was a general election that month and
she wrote Reinhardt that: 'I have recorded my vote but with the
utmost reluctance. All three parties stink in decent nostrils, and

have done their best to sicken the electorate, not only by their unfailing duplicity, but by their stupid tactics (maddening one and all by Permeating the Air night after night) and by their wearisome mudslinging. As for the Gentleman Downstairs, you can Have Him – synthetic smile and all.' Edward Heath had chambers below theirs and she sometimes found his piano playing a little trying, though relations were superficially friendly enough. She was later to describe him as 'the most deplorable Prime Minister that our country has had to endure since Lord North lost the American Colonies'. When she did make a political statement, it was a strong one. But she undoubtedly voted Conservative this time. She always did except for one memorable occasion in 1945 when the Labour Party promised great things for the arts and she voted Labour and was never let forget it by her resident males.

By April she could give Reinhardt an outline of *Black Sheep*, calling it: 'A singularly useless description of this meretricious work.' It is one of her longer and less brilliant synopses, but ends with a characteristic description of her hero, the Black Sheep himself:

He is not going to be a typical Heyer-hero – suave, well-dressed, rich, and a famous whip, according to Model No. 1; or, Model No. 2, the brusque, savage sort, with a foul temper. He *is* very rich, but as he has not the slightest wish to cut a dash no one suspects it . . . I expect he amassed his fortune in the easy thoroughly shady way which all the nabobs, as far as I can discover, did in India.

At some point over the years, she had changed the order of her heroes. Mark I used to be the brusque, savage one. Now, she urged Reinhardt to 'play up my outrageous hero!'

Their lease of the Albany chambers ran out in 1966, and they decided to move as the access stairs were becoming too much for her. She wrote from Greywalls in August that they had found a flat in Jermyn Street and hoped to move in September: 'It has constant hot water, and central heating, and if I had Domestic Difficulty I could run it with one hand tied behind me.' Back in London, she was soon hard at work turning out the accumulations of their twenty-five years at Albany, and planning a 'house-cooling' cocktail party. She was in good heart, writing in mock despair of the piles of spare copies of her books that must be got rid of before the move, and ending: 'My Life's Companion, practically born and bred in Russia, has suddenly Put his Foot Down, and uttered a Decree! – There must be plenty of Caviar – and the best fresh caviar – at the party, and on No Account must it be served in Disgusting Pastry Boats . . . He has waltzed off to Wisbech for the entire week, but did, at least, order the Proper Vodka before he left my side.'

She was invited to an informal lunch at Buckingham Palace in November, the Master of the Household telling her that they were all 'Madly Keen' on her books. She described the occasion in a letter to an old friend: 'My dear, it was the *oddest* party! There were ten or twelve guests, and I was the only Female!!! . . . However it was all very easy, but also funny. Carola Oman says I ought to have foreseen that the Queen would be terrified of me, because Royals are always frightened of Inkies.' But the Queen's '*ordinary* voice' was far better than her broadcasting one, and she had 'a merry twinkle and quite a lively sense of the ridiculous'. As for the Duke, on whose right hand Georgette Heyer inevitably sat at lunch: 'Well, I don't like him. I am at one with George IV, who spoke of "these damned Saxe-Coburgs!" But, give the devil his due, he is very conversible – even if he is far more aware of his "charm" than I am!' They had discussed 'certain aspects of the Western Highlands, Public Schools (with particular reference to Gordonstoun), Athleticism, and the Deadlines of Race Meetings . . .' Neither Queen nor Duke made any mention of Georgette Heyer's books 'for which – since I hate talking about my books – I was thankful. But they certainly *ought* to have done so, don't you think?'

It made a splendid story for her step-grandsons, who were amazed to hear that the royal corgis had irrupted on to the before-lunch drinks session and jumped all over both Queen and guests, but Georgette Heyer 'could only feel, like the old woman in the nursery rhyme, "Lawks-a-mussy on me, This is none of I!" Ronald, of course, is in a state of euphoria about the whole thing, but *I* think,' said his faithful wife, 'it would have been more to the point if *he* had been invited. He does far more for the Queen than I shall ever do.' Lunching with Max Reinhardt to describe the occasion, she told him she had learnt from her friends at Harrods that the Queen had been there afterwards to order a dozen copies of *Frederica* and remarked that she had found her '*very* formidable'. 'Do you think I could terrify *anyone*?' she asked him now, in her loud clear voice, terrifying every waiter.

Things were going better and better in the United States. Her agent, Joyce Weiner, had gone there in 1965, found 'a staggering amount of interest' in her work, and stimulated Dutton into a mass issue of previously unpublished back titles. *The Conqueror*, *Devil's Cub*, *The Convenient Marriage* and *The Corinthian*, which had previously been published in the United States as *Beau Wyndham* in 1941, all came out in the autumn of 1966, together with *Regency Buck*. Dutton pulled out all the stops, jacketing *The Conqueror* in a reproduction of part of the Bayeux Tapestry to point up the fact that 1966 marked the 900th anniversary of the Battle of Hastings, and celebrating the event with a full-page advertisement in the *New York Times*. Paperback sales were soaring in the United States, too, in those days when every drug store had its rack of mixed romance and adventure. In fact, the Dutton reprinting of the back titles had been precipitated by Bantam Books' offer for them. But Putnam, Georgette Heyer said, were 'sitting on a lot of my titles . . . keeping them in print by selling the paperback rights to Ace Books, which must be the worst paperback company ever seen!' The trouble here was partly that since she had left Christy & Moore she had no permanent representative in the United States to protect her interests and keep her in the picture.

In England, the Penguin *False Colours* came out that autumn and she hated its jacket: 'Cheap and nasty. Pan . . . used to

The New York Times *advertisement, 30 October 1966. Dutton issued six titles at once, and celebrated the anniversary of the Battle of Hastings by using the Bayeux Tapestry for the jacket of* The Conqueror.

produce this kind of thing under the mistaken impression that a "suggestive" picture helped sales – until I showed them that they much mistook the matter! The People who like my books, and those who *will* like them, are not at all attracted by lush and abandoned females on the wrapper. Pan are now sending me sketches for proposed wrappers, [and] producing really classy jobs, which are most attractive, and they are certainly not losing by it.' She was never too busy to care about this aspect of her work. Penguin let her see the proposed new jacket for *False Colours* when they reprinted it in 1967 and she approved its abstract design without enthusiasm: 'I did suggest that it was a trifle dim, and would hardly strike people as being an advertisement for any book of mine. I was told that the firm was now adopting a policy of Quiet Elegance – ! Also (rather loftily) that all my previous jackets had been on the vulgar side. You know, Max, I was lost in admiration of myself! I did NOT say, "Well, yours certainly was!" and I did not recommend the gentleman to look at my new Pan books.' But she stayed with Pan.

Black Sheep came out in December and did well. It combined the warmer tone of her later books with the neat plotting of some of the early ones, and was, of course, the book she had spoken of as far back as October 1964, when she was struggling with *Frederica* and said that she was being distracted by 'plans for the next, and *much* more amusing book'. Like *A Civil Contract*, therefore, it had had a longer incubation period than usual and had gained by it. It has a characteristic double plot, with the Black Sheep's wooing of Abigail Wendover counterpointed by his nephew Stacy's unsuccessful pursuit of her niece. The two themes are beautifully interwoven, with just one uncharacteristic slip where Miles Calverleigh is seen setting a snare for his worthless nephew some twenty pages after Stacy has fallen into it. But this serves mainly as a reminder of how brilliantly Georgette Heyer normally keeps her various threads in hand, sliding imperceptibly from one character to another.

Miles Calverleigh, her 'outrageous hero', is as intriguing as she prophesied, and Abigail an independent-minded heroine in the vein of Ancilla in *The Nonesuch* only more deeply drawn. For once, her independent mind is her own; she owes nothing to her father. Georgette Heyer was taking a new look at her world in this book. She had abandoned the aristocracy for the moneyed middle classes, and money is the dominant theme, with class a close second. But even money is no longer everything. More than ever, the manners and morals are those of the heart. They go deep. And the comedy is quieter, with more of the ironic Jane Austen vein, as in the treatment of Selina, the *malade imaginaire* sister who clings to Abigail and does her best to prevent her marriage to Miles. In the end, having turned the money theme upside down, Georgette Heyer treats herself to her first completed elopement, or, to be precise, abduction. Miles, seeing Abigail an exhausted martyr to her selfish sister, carries her off, protesting:

'Stop *at once*! If you think I am going to elope with you—'

'No, no!' he said. 'This isn't an elopement! I'm abducting you!'

She tried to speak, but dared not trust her voice.

'I thought it would be the best thing to do,' he explained.

That was too much for her self-control; for the life of her she could not help bursting into laughter.

Laughter, like sunlight, has broken in again.

They had moved to their Jermyn Street flat in the last week of November, and Georgette Heyer described the move in a letter to a friend a few days later. 'Ronald had the brilliant idea of moving all the books and pictures a week before the furniture – and had planned to take last week "off", but press of legal business intervened, and the Dear Little Man was not, as you might say, Amongst us! *Men* – ! As I've had to line my study almost to the ceiling with shelves, most of the adjusting of shelves and fitting in of the books was done at the top of a pair of steps – and I rapidly discovered that to carry more than a few volumes at a time results in a Cascade, and severe loss of temper!' They had the decorators in, and by the middle of December she came down with 'a shocking attack of tracheitis, which has left me exhausted, but still Amongst You. I feel remote from Literature, but I've been playing with an idea for the next book.' Tracheitis, translated, is inflammation of the throat. She had suffered from what was diagnosed as streptococcal throat before, and would die of cancer of the lungs eight years later. She habitually smoked sixty to eighty cork-tipped cigarettes a day, maintaining always that she did not inhale. But the connection had not then been strongly made, and the warning signs were ignored.

The enthusiastic reviews of *Black Sheep* meant a new series of requests for interviews. One of these particularly irritated Georgette Heyer and is typical of the kind of thing she had to endure. From a journalist who has since established herself, it was addressed to Heinemann instead of The Bodley Head, and one ill-typed paragraph read: 'I expect people gabble about how they've read all your books, when you [*sic*] ask to interview you. I haven't – I've never read *The Talisman Ring*. If I can explain – I haven't read all the rest *because* I wanted to interview you. I wanted to interview you because I'd read them all several times since I discovered *Powder and Patch* in the school gymnasium lavatories.'

Georgette Heyer was able to resist this illiterate request. They went to Venice for Easter 1967, staying, as they always did, at Cipriani's. Back in England, she made one of her rare political remarks: 'Isn't it FUN to see the Israelis beating hell out of the Wogs? . . . All the same, I wish I could see a solution to the problem, but I can't. It looks like another uneasy truce in a Hundred Years' War.'

Ronald received the CBE for his work on the General Optical Council that summer and his wife was delighted: 'At least R. got it for something worth while.' Carola Oman had received the CBE in 1957, also for something worth while. Once again, Georgette Heyer can hardly have failed to make a quiet personal comparison. Back from Greywalls in the autumn, she produced a stirring outline for *Cousin Kate*. It is worth quoting whole, since this one time the proposal, sadly, is better than the book:

Cousin Kate is the orphaned daughter of an impoverished Peninsular officer. Her mother died years ago, and she followed the drum with Pop. He must have been a very volatile

A page of carriages from the notebooks. Georgette Heyer was expert in the niceties of riding and driving.

type, because, when he died (of natural causes, *after* Waterloo), he left her with nothing but debts. I expect he was a gamester, or Lived Above his Income, but I'll work that out later. Don't interrupt! Well, there the poor girl was, aged 23, and reduced to Penury, in an age where females couldn't waltz out, and Get a Job as easy as drop your hat. So when her dimly-remembered aunt-by-marriage, Lady (Minerva) Brede, invited her to Seek a Loving Asylum at Lynwood, the seat of Sir Timothy Brede, Minerva's aged and fairly doddering husband, she agreed to do so. This is where the book begins. What the reader doesn't know, and you wouldn't, unless I told you, is that Minerva, who was Poor old Sir Timothy's second wife, has a deep-laid and Dastardly plot in mind. Her only son, Torquil, the sole issue of her marriage, and the heir to the ancient baronetcy, and the Splendid Estate (somewhere in the Midlands), is rapidly developing into a homicidal, and/or suicidal maniac. He is an incredibly beautiful youth of 19, fitfully obsessed by a Persecution Complex, and believed by fond, doting father to be physically so delicate that he had to be educated at home, and couldn't be exposed to the rigours of life at either University. I shall have to introduce a bribed physician, but I know All About his smiling 'valet' already, so DO stop interrupting with quite idiotic caveats, Max! Anyway, Minerva, who is beautiful, and clever, and completely hard-boiled, knows her son is going to come to a sticky end sooner or later (and probably sooner) unless he is kept under restraint, and she conceives the happy idea of marrying him to her providentially orphaned niece-by-marriage, who has no other relations to worry about her, or to make trouble. With a son-and-heir in view, of course. After which Torquil can commit suicide without prejudicing her position as Queen Bee of Lynwood – for, naturally, the poor little friendless widow will allow herself to be dominated by her beautiful and ever-so-kind mother-in-law. Sir Timothy, you must know, is not expected to live very much longer.

Yes, I heard what you said, and *really*, Max, how can you be so dumb? *Of course* there's a Hero! Do you think I was born yesterday? He may look like the Villain of the Piece, but he's no such thing. Nor is Kate the lovely, innocent half-wit her face and her pretty manners might lead you to suppose. I don't quite know yet what will happen to Torquil: he may drown himself in the lake – I'll put one in, just in case I find I need it – but I daresay he will just be put under the aforementioned restraint. It doesn't much matter, so I'll let things take their own course.

It's no use sicking Barbosa on to me. The only idea in my head, for a jacket, is a Sylvan Scene, on the bridge thrown across the narrow end of the lake, with poor, beautiful Torquil gazing down into the water. With or with not, Kate standing beside him.

She warned Reinhardt that 'I do NOT know when this book will be finished. Damn it, I haven't *started* it yet! But I don't propose to waste much time on it, and I trust that nothing will crop up to interrupt its progress.'

But something did. She had flu, and 'the worst cold of the century' that winter, but by January 1968 she could tell Belinda Westcott at Bodley Head that she had 'done about 30,000 words of *Cousin Kate*, and they stink. I don't suppose you've ever been subjected to a course of diuretics, but I can assure you that they have the most disintegrating effect. I am reduced to dust and ashes, and have no wit in me.' Her trouble had been more than flu. She ended this letter: 'I will end, in mediaeval style, by wishing you long life and well-enduring.' She must have been thinking about her cherished mediaeval project again while she wrestled with the side-effects of the diuretics.

She finished *Cousin Kate* at last in April, writing Reinhardt: 'I hope to finish Accursed Kate this week . . . Do you want a blurb for it? Here's one for you: "This dreary romance, we confidently predict, will disappoint Miss Heyer's many admirers. It is almost totally devoid of wit, or, in fact, interest. It is not even well written; and will, we believe, become a valuable addition to the library, as the worst book she has ever written. Order your copy now!"' A week later, she described the actual finishing of the book: 'At 4.00 this morning. Owing to my having, some weeks ago, rewritten and retyped quite a number of pages . . . *and* owing to the trifling difficulty caused by the fact that the numbering of the pages had gone haywire . . . And when wildly searching for the correct page, I kept on mixing up the three copies, and altogether it was a hellish night! Warn the printer to pay no heed to my page-numbering! I'm too tired to renumber the 498 pages, so if he gets them muddled, he'll have had it!' She did have secretarial help, but never, perhaps, enough. And she had worn herself out finishing *Cousin Kate*. 'Do you know, for seven worrying nights after I'd sent off Accursed Kate I dreamed that I hadn't finished the thing, and kept on composing sentences, and weird new endings!'

Belinda Westcott, Max Reinhardt's assistant, had tried her hand at her first blurb for *Cousin Kate*, and got a firm answer. 'No, no, Belinda! – I'm sorry, but it won't do! The one thing a blurb should *not* do is to divulge the entire plot of a book. My husband is quite incendiary about this . . . I don't want to sound insufferable, but I know from the various booksellers of my acquaintance that when it comes to selling ME, no one wants to know what my latest is About: they only want to know whether there is a new Heyer Out.' She enclosed an admirable brief blurb of her own, which Bodley Head used verbatim.

The book came out in September, while the Rougiers were at Greywalls, and went straight to the top of the best-seller lists. Georgette Heyer had been quite right about her avid public, but the book does show signs of the 'quite ghastly disabilities' under which she wrote it. Orphaned Kate is an engaging, capable heroine, and the lower-class Nidds who befriend her a well-drawn group of cockneys, but the hero is a mere shadow of a Heyer Model II and the bad characters a set of cardboard cut-outs. Lady Broome's[1] obsession with the Staplewood estate comes over well, but her son Torquil's madness fails totally to convince. For once in her life, his creator had not done quite enough homework on this. As if to make up for it, and the slightness of the plot, she over-indulged herself in detail of

1 Since writing the synopsis Georgette Heyer has changed her name from Brede to Broome.

clothes, and food, and architecture, while the Nidds' slang passes all bounds. The laughter is rare in this book, and sometimes forced, and the whole tone just slightly sick. Was Georgette Heyer intentionally trying her hand at the contemporary Gothic, or did this simply reflect her own poor state of health?

Another continuing problem had been that of Heron Enterprises. Her new accountant, Hale Crosse, had been urging her to sell her unlucky company to Booker McConnell, the huge international company that already owned the Ian Fleming and Agatha Christie estates, and would later fund the Booker Prize for fiction. Always averse to change, she and Ronald had taken almost two years to come round to this idea. At last, Hale Crosse was allowed to bring two Booker directors to meet the Rougiers over a drink, and after some initial resistance (Georgette Heyer actually pretended at first that they had come on the wrong day) the directors proved agreeable and the economic argument overwhelming, and the thing was done at last. 'This has been a long and wearing business,' she wrote, 'but it has ended extremely satisfactorily. Booker's are very nice people to deal with, and I like the three men who have been appointed directors. On my side, there's Me, and my husband, and my son.' Ronald was ill, but Richard 'shot up from his Gloucestershire home to support me at the Grand Lunch given at Bucklersbury House to seal the contract, and went over very big with his fellow-directors! It was very funny, for we had a Board Meeting first – Richard and me, the three Booker's directors, my solicitor, Booker's solicitor, my accountant and their accountant, at which we signed and exchanged documents, and three Enormous cheques were solemnly handed over to me . . . Then we all went to lunch . . . and I found an orchid on my plate!!! As it is years since anyone gave me an orchid that quite made my day!'

The three enormous cheques were for herself, Ronald and Richard. As directors of Heron Enterprises they shared the purchase price for the seventeen of her titles the company had owned. The total was in the region of £85,000 and had the advantage of coming to them at low capital transfer rather than high income tax rates. Characteristically, the Rougiers' shares were put on bank deposit. They were always reluctant to invest money, partly from natural inertia, partly for fear of unexpected tax demands. Thanks to their new accountant, these were now a thing of the past, but the expected ones continued painful. From now on Georgette Heyer's earnings for the rest of her titles ran at about £60,000 to £70,000 a year, but it was never quite enough. Meticulous to a fault, she disappointed Hale Crosse by her refusal ever to apply her mind to calculating the expenses authors are allowed to charge up against their taxes. Where most authors charge up travel expenses and so forth, she was with difficulty persuaded to charge a percentage of her telephone bill, and her London Library subscription (fourteen guineas in the late 1960s) was usually her largest expense. She had never committed the economy of making herself a life member.

She was beginning to be unhappy about the state of things at Dutton in New York. She never achieved the happy relationship with an American publisher that she had with her two favourite English ones. Even now, with American sales soaring, and fan letters flooding in, she never thought of going there, and the lack of an American agent remained a serious disadvantage. She was furious when she learnt in the autumn of 1968 that Dutton 'had the nerve to demand a photostat or some such nonsense' from The Bodley Head. 'Pay no heed to any such impertinence,' said the irate author, apparently unaware of the agreeable extent to which publishers work together across the Atlantic. She was equally amazed on one occasion when she recognized that her American edition was an exact copy of the English one, presumably another case of transatlantic co-operation. There was trouble about American copyrights, too, and she began to think seriously about getting an American agent. 'And a lawyer,' said Joyce Weiner, but nothing came of this sensible idea, though Hale Crosse was heartily in favour of it.

Richard and Susie had bought a Georgian house called Murrell's End at Redmarley in Gloucestershire, and the Rougiers spent Christmas 1968 there: 'A most enjoyable, if somewhat strenuous time! I can't tell you how lovely it was at Redmarley, with snow lying on the Malvern Hills, and on the more distant Welsh mountains, and a rural peace all round!' She had decided not to try and write a book that spring: 'Partly because I didn't want to and partly because I refuse to throw any more than I damned well must down the National Drain.' They planned to go to Iceland in July and to Greywalls as usual in August. 'Then,' she wrote to Reinhardt in April, 'I expect I'd better write another book! But I am enjoying my idle year!' But later that month she came down with another 'ghastly throat' which reminded her of the streptococcal one she had had years before.

They enjoyed Iceland. 'The country is like none I have seen anywhere . . . It's as though a giant in a very bad humour once lived underground and flung up mountains higgledy-piggledy all over the place!' In the same long letter to a friend she answered a question about politics: 'All the same, these politicians, I loathe them, and won't have one across my threshold if I can avoid it. The only one of the whole bunch who has courage, and a great many proper ideas is Enoch Powell! He also has a first-class brain, but I think he would be dangerous as the leader of a Party.' She added that she hated the new currency, abominated computers, 'And nothing will prevail upon me to use numerals in place of proper place-names.' A question about the Budget elicited another of her positive political statements: 'What disgusts me about it is the callous unconcern shown in it for the countless millions who subsist by the skin of their teeth on low incomes. The purchase tax on all household textiles is INIQUITOUS. What becomes of the young couples who have been saving up to buy the bare necessities, such as sheets, and towels, and dusters? As for clapping the extra tax on potato crisps and Kleenex hankies, I think it is contemptible.'

They had to go to Gleneagles instead of Greywalls in the summer of 1969, as there had been a fire at Greywalls and it was closed for the season. Gleneagles was so huge, she said, that guests had to be issued with a map, and it was also full of the noisier type of rich Americans, but they made friends with 'a nice

A page from Esquire, *December 1966. Members of a Georgette Heyer Fan Club in New Jersey dress up and act scenes from her novels.*

couple from Connecticut, who were so disgusted . . . by the behaviour of some of their compatriots that it was necessary from time to time to make soothing noises . . . There were also a considerable number of British *nouveaux riches*.' Altogether they were glad to move to a hotel in North Berwick where she read a couple of novels Reinhardt had sent her: 'Both these books leave me bewildered, and wondering "What's it all supposed to be about?" Ah, well! I'm a back number, believing in all sorts of outdated things.'

Reinhardt had also sent her a long article on her work by A. S. Byatt, published in *Nova*. Thanking him for it she wrote: 'I'm told that the writer of that article about me is the sister of Marjorie (?) Drabble – a name that means nothing to me, but Joyce [Weiner] seemed to think well of it. What a *horrid* publication *Nova* is!' And then, 'Of course, what stunned me was that awful Laski woman's estimate of me:[1] I shouldn't have supposed she could possibly like my work, should you?' She was to be proved right about this in the fullness of time, but it is an interesting measure of her detachment from the literary scene that she had not even heard of Margaret Drabble, who had been publishing novels steadily and with critical acclaim since *A Summer Birdcage* appeared in 1963.

Her older sister, Antonia Byatt, too, was already known as critic, don and author of serious novels and a book on Iris Murdoch. Obviously Georgette Heyer was not an avid reader of the book pages. The *Nova* article is in fact a serious, respectful and extremely interesting discussion of Georgette Heyer's work as escape literature. The fairy-tale element in the books, A. S. Byatt says, is balanced by Georgette Heyer's extraordinary accuracy of detail. In the end, she shows signs of crediting Georgette Heyer with something more than escapism: 'She is playing romantic games with the novel of manners. In her world of 'romanticized anti-romanticism . . . men and women really

1 In her article, A.S. Byatt says: 'Marghanita Laski has said that Georgette Heyer is a genius and defies description.'

White Horse Cellar, Piccadilly, by Cruikshank: 'Coaches and waggons to all parts of the Kingdom'. Quality used their own carriages, and heroes like Sir Richard Wyndham in The Corinthian *and Sylvester suffered rude awakenings when reduced to public transport.*

talk to each other . . . and plan to spend the rest of their lives together developing the relationship.' And, finally: 'In her romantic novels, as in Jane Austen's, it is love the people are looking for, and love they give each other.' It is sad not to have Georgette Heyer's reaction to this perceptive comment.

By November she was writing again, and 'Quite Enjoying myself! . . . I think what I've done is Quite Good! Anyway, it is – to judge by Ronald's chuckles – quite amusing! Certain developments are still undecided but I have always found that when I can't make up my mind whether or not to make this or that happen the only thing to do is to start writing the book, and allow the later events in it to grow on their own. Of course this does sometimes lead to a ghastly period in the middle, when one can't think what to do next; but it frequently leads to no problem at all, one's characters deciding the matter without any assistance from their author.'

Progress was stopped at 35,000 words before Christmas by what she called 'One of my Queer Turns'. These happened, she said, when she was asleep, and resulted from a momentary failure of the main artery to the brain, due to an awkward position of her head. She hoped to solve it by putting blocks under the head of her bed, and went to Murrell's End for Christmas, but came back very tired and in need of a strong tonic. Just the same, she had written 60,000 words by the end of January. 'In record time, too, which I didn't think I was still capable of doing!' she wrote a friend. She promised Reinhardt March delivery: 'The Title is *Charity Girl*, and the period towards the end of the second decade of the XIXth Century. The mixture as before, in fact . . . Now that my hand is "in" I think I'll write another book and have already begun to plan it. It would be a nice experience to write a book with plenty of time on hand – and I have got an Idea! It seems to me that I'd better make hay while the sun shines and before I become entirely decrepit . . . While I can work, I bloody well will!'

She was worrying again about the American scene that winter. Writing to Reinhardt before he left for a trip to New York

Georgette Heyer. The last formal photograph, taken for The Times *in 1970. Her first impulse when approached about this was to say she was just off to the South Pole.*

in January 1970, she told him that she expected to see her American editor in London shortly, so 'Perhaps you better 'adn't do any whispering. And it wouldn't do any good if you *shouted* my opinion of Putnam's.' But she hoped Reinhardt would bring her back, 'Whatever dope you've picked up in New York about Putnam's and Ace Books – whose souls God pardon!' It does sound as if she needed an American agent. But she was getting on better with Bantam Books, who were now sending her jacket sketches as Pan did, 'with excellent results!'

With *Charity Girl* at the printers, she was able to report to Joyce Weiner in May that its subscription was already well up on *Cousin Kate*'s figures at the same stage. She had lunched with Frere who had told her that her publisher's only problem had always been whether to print 'A first edition of 40, 50 or 60 thousand copies! I still don't entirely believe him.' In fact, she was being modest as usual. In an interview in *The Bookseller* Frere had quoted figures of 80, 90, or 100,000 copies. All her life, she needed constant reassurance about her sales. And she was appalled at the price Bodley Head meant to charge for *Charity Girl*. Reinhardt had to explain that costs were 'sky-rocketing, and 30/- for a novel is considered very reasonable nowadays.' Translated to £1.50 in modern terms it seems very reasonable indeed.

Ronald, always the more enthusiastic traveller, urged a cruise of the Norwegian fjords that summer. She resisted at first: 'Not being at all fond of sea voyages, I suggested that he should find himself a Nice Blonde, and take her instead of me, but he says he's too old for Nice Blondes!' Ronald was still very busy with various chairmanships, though he had retired from the Bar itself. Just as well, his wife said, 'For he's the type of man who is never well when he has nothing to do.' She went to Norway, of course, and summed it up in a quotation: '"Where every prospect pleases, and only man is vile"'. Afterwards they went to Greywalls as usual, but she wrote from there that she had been 'smitten on the journey by some sort of virus', and was suffering from blocked eustachian tubes. *Charity Girl* was to be published on 1 October, and in September she received a letter from

Michael Ratcliffe, the literary editor of *The Times*, asking if she would agree to be photographed for an article about her work that Marghanita Laski was writing. He ended his letter: 'I fully understand your reticence, particularly since we "quality" newspapers have not exactly devoted a vast amount of space to your work in the past few years, but we do promise to make amends and Marghanita is doing her homework very thoroughly.'

Her first impulse was to say that she was just off to the South Pole, 'But Ronald has persuaded me to give way. He says I really *must* be photographed just once more, or there won't be a photograph of me for my obituary notice!' When Miss Laski's piece, complete with photograph, appeared on 1 October, she must have wished she had stuck to her lifelong rule. She had been promised a sight of the picture, but did not get it, and the one *The Times* used shows her evidently hating the whole business. The article, titled 'The Appeal of Georgette Heyer', was in fact a four-column sneer at once at the books, their readers and, by implication, their author. If Miss Laski had once thought Georgette Heyer a genius who defied description she had changed her mind. The article drew enraged letters from fans, and the suggestion that Miss Laski was 'consumed by jealousy'. Or had she simply failed to re-read the books? It was a sad episode, but did not affect *Charity Girl*'s place on the best-seller lists.

Georgette Heyer had been right when she described it as 'the mixture as before', and fans who had been upset by the unexpected element of nastiness in *Cousin Kate* must have been relieved. It is set squarely back in the private world, with new variations on a couple of familiar themes. Viscount Desford, a pleasant example of the Model II hero, has never realized he is in love with his old friend Hetta, but instinctively turns to her for help when he gets involved with a runaway beauty, who is neither quite so beautiful nor quite so stupid as Belinda in *The Foundling* and has none of the backbone of Amanda in *Sprig Muslin*. The slight plot is enlivened by some admirable scenes and strong characters. Cherry, the Charity Girl, is modelled on

Harriet Smith in *Emma*, while her appalling if highly entertaining father owes a great deal to Dickens's sanctimonious villains. And there are some engaging, and unusual, sidelights on married life. Desford has a gout-ridden irascible old papa, who might easily have resembled the tyrants in *Penhallow* and *The Unknown Ajax*, but not a bit of it; all his household are fond of the old tartar. 'I remember how gay, and handsome, and dashing he used to be, and how very happy we were,' says his still loving wife. This is a happy book, full of mellow laughter, even if it does have the occasional repetition, a little too much slang, and, for once, some slightly jolting changes of subject.

Dutton had their own plans for the promotion of *Charity Girl*. They thought of sending one of Georgette Heyer's American fans to Bath, where it was set. If they did, would she meet the fan for a drink at the Ritz? Her refusal was entirely predictable, and her impatience with Dutton increased. She and Ronald were used to such velvet-gloved handling from first Heinemann and then Bodley Head that the more casual American approach inevitably came as a shock. Meticulous civility to her publisher was her own watchword. She expected to have her letters answered and could not accommodate to the American habit of settling everything by telephone. It was a generation gap as well as a transatlantic one. And she was not getting milder with advancing age. There had been a brief but formidable explosion when she thought Bodley Head were interfering in her long and happy relationship with her jacket designer, Barbosa.

Her health was far from good that winter. She had never quite shaken off the infection that had troubled her at Greywalls, and by December she was on antibiotics for her throat as well as diuretics for a swollen foot. There was no talk of a book that winter, and she wrote gloomily about a dustmen's strike and the threat of power cuts. But the sales of *Charity Girl* were cheering, and a royalty cheque for over £13,000 in April drew a pleased response: 'I shan't be going into the workhouse this year, shall I?' She added that she was 'a good deal better', and that they were flying to Venice for an Aegean cruise in May. Before they went

Cocking at the Royal Cockpit, by Cruikshank. Peregrine Taverner, in Regency Buck, *was provoked to a duel at the only cockfight Georgette Heyer ever described.*

they had to fill in their census form: 'Ronald quietly removed it from me, and filled it in, knowing that I couldn't be trusted not to get funny about it.' She enjoyed the cruise, and particularly loved Rhodes, but on their last day in Venice she forgot to take off her bifocals when getting into one of Cipriani's water-taxis, misjudged the distance and gashed her right leg badly. She was afraid she would still be a semi-cripple when they went to Greywalls in August.

Joyce Weiner retired that year, and recommended that she go to Deborah Owen, American wife of the politician, David Owen, who had recently set up her own small agency. Before making the decision, Georgette Heyer asked to meet David Owen, explaining that a wife was incomplete without her husband. It was impossible to know her without knowing him. Having decided that 'your Life's Companion [a favourite phrase of hers] . . . is definitely a charmer', she was soon teasing Deborah Owen for being American like the fans who wrote her gushing letters on deplorable writing paper. Once again, business relationship turned to friendship. The Rougiers dined with the Owens in their house on the Thames in dockland and lunched with them at the House of Commons, where it was Ronald who was recognized, by Dick Taverne, as 'the outstanding barrister'.

Deborah Owen, who had been terrified of meeting her formidable new author, was soon getting friendly 'Dear Debbie' letters about everything from colds by way of the new book to grandchildren. She felt that Georgette Heyer might actually enjoy a little more contact with the publishing world, and did contrive a meeting between her and her editor at Pan, who had always wanted to see his elusive author in the flesh. Impressed by the immense style with which she talked, Deborah Owen thought she would have been happiest as the one woman member of a men's dining club.

The Jermyn Street flat had proved a disappointment, a kind of imitation Albany without enough space or view, and they moved again that autumn, as always renting rather than buying. Georgette Heyer wrote that she was 'being driven mental by the apparent inability of so-called first-class firms either to listen to what one tells them or to read typed instructions.' But by November they were more or less settled at 28 Parkside, Knightsbridge. It was a seventh-floor flat, spacious and quiet, overlooking Hyde Park on one side and Knightsbridge on the other, and 'We are both sure that we are going to like the new flat very much.'

Their Christmas was not going to be a very festive occasion as Frank Heyer's wife had just died and Boris's was seriously ill. But 'I am more or less restored to health; Ronald is fit; and Richard and his family are all in Rude Health.' Ronald had now retired from all legal activities, but would keep on the Chairmanship of the General Optical Council for another year. 'This will let him down lightly,' wrote his wife. 'But I view the future with a certain amount of misgiving. He is one of those who can't thrive unless his brain is fully occupied.' She was also a little sad because they had rather lost touch with their dear friends the Freres, but she was longing to see the Reinhardts, 'And to remember that I am not only a Sister, and a Housewife, but a NOVELIST as well! At the moment, I am too tired even to think about a new book, but this has happened to me many times before, and I know that suddenly an Idea will burst on me – after which I shall forget that I'm a Sister and a Housewife, and shall plunge deep into the early XIXth Century, and be lost to Society until I have written THE END!'

Chapter 10

*T*he Rougiers celebrated the move to Knightsbridge with a party at the end of January 1972. They expected fifty to sixty people: 'I can only hope that we don't burst at the seams!' Georgette Heyer wrote Reinhardt. She was worrying about finance again: 'The thing which bothers me is Death Duties! And they do bother me, considerably more than somewhat.' But, 'I'll wait until my party is behind me before plunging into business.' She never did do anything about Death Duties.

That January a letter from an American who was belatedly reviewing *The Conqueror* got the usual answer: 'I have the greatest dislike of Personal Publicity; and . . . have never been able to understand what my private life has to do with my novels . . . I can't but feel that it would be profoundly depressing to my youthful fans, who seem (from their letters) to be convinced that my Ideal Man is the prototype of what I call the Heyer Hero, No. I pattern – a horrid type, whom no woman in the possession of her senses could endure for more than half a day. He doesn't occur in the *Conqueror*, which is probably why that book is not amongst my best-sellers.'

Soon after the house-warming party, she fell, fractured a fibula, and 'became once again house-bound!' Recovering, she wrote a friend that she had been 'forced to apply what little inventive brain I still have to the writing of a book, at breakneck speed, for autumn publication, and went into strict retirement. This effort left me entirely exhausted.' She was basically unwell

The coffee shop, by Cruikshank. Regency young men foregathered here, but no lady might darken its doors.

in her later years, fighting it gallantly, but throwing out accidents like symptoms. Once again, she would not spare herself and miss her publisher's deadline. She only did that once in her long writing life, over *Frederica*, in 1964.

She finally sent Reinhardt her outline of *Lady of Quality* at the end of April. Unlike the one for *Cousin Kate*, this rather pedestrian blurb does the book less than justice, and her husband was wise to suggest, as she told Reinhardt, that Bodley Head stress the fact that the hero was 'the rudest man in London'. She sent detailed advice about the jacket design with the blurb: 'Miss Wychwood is a dazzling blonde – corn-coloured, not flaxen! Upper Camden Place, where she lived, is now known as Camden Crescent, and . . . part of this Crescent, curving up from the bottom left . . . would make an admirable cover design . . . the houses, built (I think) of Bath Stone, are extremely elegant . . . I'm not much in favour of introducing the Hero into the picture, but if you and the artist decide otherwise, he is dark, with a swarthy complexion. Mr Carleton, of course! Didn't you GUESS?' It was no wonder her publishers loved her. Nearly seventy, she was still professional through and through.

She went on to describe her progress with the book: 'I've left

[Carleton] making himself thoroughly obnoxious to Lord Beckenham, in the Pump Room, and must go back to him, and think of a few more poisonously rude things for him to say. What was that you said? How is it all going to end? Do be your age, Max! How on earth can I know? I do know that Miss Wychwood is going to horrify her relations by marrying Mr Carleton; and I rather think that Lucilla will end up by marrying Harry Beckenham – but probably not within the scope of this book. Anyway, what does it matter? I have only to add that Mr Carleton is not merely the rudest man in London, but has also the reputation of being a Sad Rake, to convince you that he has all the right ingredients of a Heyer-Hero.' Signing this, 'Yours, to my little power', she sounds herself again, and the typed letter is an indication that she was at work. A woman who liked everything handsome about her, she had bought herself an elaborate and efficient Norwegian writing desk, back at Albany, and when she installed her typewriter on it for a book there was no room to write by hand.

Since the trouble over *Cousin Kate*, when a page got lost in her late-night collating, Bodley Head were getting her copy retyped for her, and she delivered fifty to sixty thousand words before she and Ronald left for Aviemore and then Greywalls for Whitsun. She thought there were about twenty thousand words still to be written: 'And it won't take long to polish them off – now that a Light has Dawned on me. It dawned quite suddenly, this afternoon, at the eleventh hour, in fact! Until that thrice blessed moment I really didn't know how to end the book for the only ending I could think of was so unsatisfactory that I grew more and more depressed. And then it came to me! . . . I foresee no more difficulties . . . But it is high time I got away for a brief respite, for I am very tired.' In a postscript she added that she had 'read what I've written to Ronald, and he assures me it's not at all dull'.

She needed this reassurance. She wrote Joyce Weiner that she kept getting 'bogged down' in this book and described it, as so often, as a 'real STINKER'. Bodley Head had scheduled it for

October publication and she finished it at last at high speed in mid-June, with Max Reinhardt himself rushing her copy to the printer. To add to their troubles, Barbosa, who had designed her jackets for so long, was ill, and Bodley Head had to find another artist who would do a jacket in his style. Thanks to Georgette Heyer's precise instructions, this one, by Edward Mortelmans, turned out to be 'one of the best jackets I've yet had, and almost indistinguishable from Barbosa's best'.

Ronald's retirement must have meant a diminution in their income, and the tax wolf was at the door again. She wrote Reinhardt in June to ask for the £10,000 advance he had promised for *Lady of Quality*. 'When I grandly said I didn't want £10,000 I was reckoning without the Treasury Sharks. It has now been borne in on me that I shall have to pour another £6,000 down the National Drain on the 1st July. This will bring the total of what I've had to pay this year to £28,000 . . . I can't tell you how MUCH I enjoy working myself to a standstill for the privilege of Educating the Masses, subsidizing the cost of strikes, and all the other things public money is squandered on.' Her conclusion was a brave one: 'Obviously I shall have to revert to the One-Book-A-Year routine.' Their combined incomes were still large, but so were their expenses. Hale Crosse had now been told to call her 'George', though he still found himself calling Ronald 'sir'. But good friend though he was, he could not overcome their built-in resistance over their tax affairs. It was hard to get papers out of them, whether publishers' statements or bills to be charged up as expenses. They hated the whole business, and would not understand it.

They went to Devon in July, but returned early, 'the rivers being far too high and muddy for fishing. Ronald did catch a few small trout, which I had for breakfast, and he learned a lot of valuable lessons from the instructor.' She went on to ask Reinhardt to thank the various people who had had the handling of her 'very messy typescript . . . And to you also my thanks for your quite Divine Patience with your tiresome author!' It was handsomely put. Most publishers would be prepared to be

Balloon ascent at Oxford, 1810. 'I do Want little Felix to be carried off in a balloon,' wrote Georgette Heyer. 'I must pay a visit to the London Library, to mug up the early balloons.'

patient with an author who steadily sold 70,000 copies in hard-back. Writing to congratulate her on her seventieth birthday that August, Reinhardt told her that they expected to do this with *Lady of Quality* and went on to tell her that *Simon the Coldheart* was in great demand among antiquarian booksellers. From time to time, fans wrote asking about the suppressed titles but Georgette Heyer was firm. She had wanted them suppressed, and suppressed they must remain.

They celebrated her seventieth birthday with champagne at Greywalls on 16 August and their forty-seventh wedding anniversary two days later with a brace of grouse. Back in London, *Lady of Quality* came out in October and *The Times* made honourable amends for the Laski article with a review by Philippa Toomey. While pointing out the strong likeness between *Lady of Quality* and *Black Sheep*, she concluded: 'Some of it is very funny, the characters are affectionately drawn, and there is, this time, that "bat's squeak of sexuality", an ingredient hitherto claimed to be missing from Miss Heyer as from Miss Austen; though it can be heard by those whose ears are adjusted to the correct frequency. *Lady of Quality* is the same again. But did anyone ever complain of being given *another* pretty little present by Fabergé?'

It was charmingly put, and fans would agree, though *Lady of Quality* is indeed close twin to *Black Sheep* and a quiet book with a minimum of plot. Georgette Heyer had been right to be anxious about the ending; the book does lose momentum about three-quarters of the way through. And there is one really failed scene where the rudest man in London is supposed to have behaved intolerably to the heroine and in fact has merely flashed a contemptuous smile and left her party early. Once again, this book would have benefited from the light hand of an editor, but it would have been a bold editor who tried.

Lady of Quality begins with a fine twist to the elopement theme. This time it is the heroine, not the hero, who rescues a runaway couple. And, like Tom and Phoebe in *Sylvester*, they are running away from marriage, not to it. Their sub-plot hardly develops, but each of them learns something from their experience with the strong-minded heroine. As she grew older, Georgette Heyer's heroes grew ruder, and her heroines both older too and more interesting. In this book the theme, as always, is love, but wound in with it is a look at the problems of the intelligent single woman. Annis is twenty-nine. Her coachman thinks her an old maid, but 'Her admirers – and she had a host of them – declared her to be a piece of perfection, and from the top of her guinea-gold curls to the soles of her slender feet they could detect no flaw in her.' She has refused to marry anyone 'for whom she felt nothing more than a mild liking' and begins to think she may dwindle into an old maid, but draws the line at becoming the kind of taken-for-granted maiden aunt Jane Austen was. Luckily for her, she is rich in her own right, so she has defied convention and set up house in Bath, burdened only with an intolerable tattling companion very much in the vein of Miss Bates, only more so. She finds in rude Oliver Carleton the laughing, loving, arguing companion she needs, and then Beatrice/Benedick relationship is beautifully done, with patches of vintage Heyer dialogue.

If the group of young characters are little more than sketches of pleasantly familiar models, the older ones are unusually interesting. More than any of the others, this book is a discussion of marriage as a reality beyond the happy ending. Annis's search for her ideal life's companion is thrown into strong relief by her brother's marriage to adoring, silly Amabel, who, significantly, is happy talking domestic nothings with Miss Farlow, the dreadful companion. Amabel's husband is a masterly portrait of the early nineteenth-century male chauvinist, his refusal to go with his suffering son to the dentist a reminder of the sharp essay Georgette Heyer wrote all those years ago about 'Fathers'. And Ninian's father is one of Georgette Heyer's domestic tyrants, as in *Penhallow* and *The Unknown Ajax*, though he and his wife exercise only 'the tyranny of the weak' over their son. There is always a strong, Johnsonian vein of realism running below the light-hearted surface of Georgette Heyer's books, particularly in the area of human relationships. Her characters may talk a language never heard on land or sea, but they behave like real people. This realism forms the base of much of her best comedy, which shows pretensions depressed and hypocrisy deflated. And, despite a slight over-indulgence in slang and period detail, it is stronger than ever in this book, only the second one of hers, I think, in which it rains.

As for what Philippa Toomey called 'the bat's squeak of sexuality', it is indeed there, as always, for those with ears to hear it. Marghanita Laski said that Georgette Heyer's characters were only sewn-up rag dolls under their worked muslin skirts or daytime pantaloons, and Georgette Heyer herself was known to say that her people lived only from the waist up. They both did her work less than justice, though for very different reasons. Overt sex, like poverty and politics, was among the things she chose to leave out of her private world of manners and morals, but this does not mean she was unaware of them. She could describe poverty and politics if she wanted to, and over and over again the long light-hearted battle between hero and heroine resolves itself at last in physical contact. The *frisson* is there for those perceptive enough to recognize it. And the fact that it is only a *frisson* is probably one of the reasons for her enduring popularity. Who wants a nymph and satyr, copulating, in the foreground of a Watteau?

She was now the kind of established figure in the United States who gets advance copies of books sent to her in the hope of enthusiastic quotes. Coward McCann sent her a copy of *Caro The Fatal Passion*, a life of Lady Caroline Lamb by Henry Blyth, that November. 'I did refrain from asking what I had ever written to give them the very false idea that this work would appeal to me; but I certainly declined to give them a write-up for it.' She had had another of her significant accidents, 'an inexplicable toss (in my own dining-room)', and been laid up for a month. She had thereupon 'Got out my mediaeval book, and ever since have been toying with the idea of bringing it to an end, with the death of Henry IV. For it is definitely GOOD, Max . . .

But it is not in my usual style, and I can't make up my mind whether to publish it or no . . . If you think it would be disastrous to publish it – well, I'll still finish it, but will then put it away to be published after my death!' It was never finished, but what she had written was duly published after her death and received some sad, respectful reviews, and Bodley Head's biggest paperback sale to date. But even her brother Frank was disappointed when he discovered that it was fiction, not the straight biography he had expected.

They spent Christmas at Murrell's End that year, 'with Richard and his family, which, since his "family" ranges in age from 16 to 6 I should think would be a riot.' The happiest aspect of these declining years of her life was her relationship with the young family. Her letters are full of Richard's growing success at the Bar. She and Susie talked on the telephone every day that they did not meet, and when she was well enough she loved to see the three little boys, and enjoyed taking them shopping at her favourite Harrods. But she was very far from well. She caught bronchitis in the New Year and had to be treated with antibiotics so strong that they left her feeling wretched. She wrote Reinhardt in February that: 'I think it extremely unlikely that I shall write a book this year. At present I could no more write a book than I could stand on my head: it is as much as I can do to write a letter. As for my mediaeval work – Oh God, no! It made me feel faint even to *look* at my notes for it. I am like the man in the old Punch joke: "I sleeps well, and I eats well, but when I sees a job of work, sir, I comes over all-of-a-tremble!"' Her handwriting confirms everything she said, but she finished on her usual courageous note. Her doctor had told her that: 'If I take things very easily . . . don't let anything worry me, and don't have any more Accidents, I shall in all probability regain all my lost vitality, and perpetrate a masterpiece.' Realist as always, she adds: 'It doesn't seem at all likely to me, but you never know!'

By March she could write a friend that: 'I was able this morning to walk with Ronald to Fortnum's, through the Green Park, without feeling so tired that I had to rest on the nearest seat! Next, if this weather holds, I shall be resuming my expeditions to the Serpentine. Until I damaged my spine, R. and I used to sally forth, armed with a bag full of stale bread, and feed the ducks and the geese.'

They were planning a trip to Provence organized by her widowed brother Frank, but this would have to be cancelled if the Travel Allowance was cut. 'Never again will I go abroad with only limited means at my disposal!' she wrote Reinhardt. 'Talking of which, do you happen to know anything about VAT as it will affect me and my kind? The Customs and Excise don't seem to have a clue, but that hasn't stopped them sending me a form to fill up.' Very sensibly, she had not looked at it yet; Ronald had done that: 'All I've done has been to sign the thing.' Luckily Hale Crosse took her VAT problems off her hands and cheered her up by pointing out that she would not be charged on her foreign royalties and sales, 'These being ranked as Valuable Exports! As a considerable part of my income comes from abroad, it looks as if I shall be a gainer, which will make a nice change.'

Back from Provence, she wrote Reinhardt in May: 'I feel about Provence much as I felt about Iceland: it was extremely interesting, I wouldn't have missed it, but I don't want to go there again.' The battle with ill health went on. She had a perpetual small, dry cough and was losing weight, which pleased her. But she had a very slight stroke in July and Ronald, rather surprisingly, took her to the north of Scotland to recuperate. She grew worse there, and ended by spending three weeks in an Edinburgh nursing home. He brought her home at last by day train, and she was well enough to see Reinhardt for lunch in September, when he and Ronald and Richard congratulated each other on her good recovery. She was fighting every inch of the way, and would not admit that she was losing.

Her brother Boris died in Oxford that November and she longed to go and see him in the Radcliffe Infirmary, but, 'Neither Ronald nor my doctor will hear of it.' It was the end of another era. She had told her first story to Boris. But Frank was very much alive, settled in 'an enchanting Regency house in Budleigh Salterton'. She was not well enough to go down to Murrell's End that year, so Richard and his family stayed in their Gloucester Road flat and she 'spent a very happy, lazy day with them', and wrote a friend that Nicholas 'has become a little boy, and no longer a baby'. She had always liked little boys best, and was lucky in her three grandsons. Dominic was a demon slow bowler, Noël was mad on fishing and they were both still devoted to Richard: 'Richard was born lucky, you know.' He had taken silk two years before and was now very busy indeed. '*He* grumbles about it, but neither Susie nor I encourage this attitude.'

She described the continuing battle with ill health in a letter to a friend written in January 1974: 'I have gradually been getting back to something approaching normal. But I still don't know what on earth I should do if I hadn't got Ronald! Pass out, I think. As always, he is a tower of strength! He retired from the Bar going on for 3 years ago, and is now doing the shopping for me – or, such of it as I can't do on the telephone. I still get desperately tired if I try to do too much, but I can at least (after several unforgettable weeks!) do my own cooking again. And I still have my very reliable Daily, who has been with me now for 23 years.' She had always been a good employer, who kept her staff. But by this time she was unable even to cross Knightsbridge, so Ronald must indeed have been a tower of strength.

She had 'another of my seizures' in February. She and Ronald had both caught cold from their reliable Peggy and the doctor thought her seizure had been the result of her coughing in the night. Ronald was actually in bed with his cold, and she meant to keep him there. 'Most of his trouble springs from worry about my health! He has always been a worrier and it is mere waste of breath to try to convince him that I am not going to pass out at any moment.'

She was lonely in those last years of her life, doubtless missing the constant, stimulating contact with her publishers over a current book. Joyce Weiner and Deborah Owen both remember enormously long telephone calls, and Deborah Owen sometimes recognized a cry for company and went straight to see her. In the spring of 1974 they learned that the well-known romantic novelist who had plagiarized her in the late Forties was at it again. A book published a year or so earlier had combined plot elements and proper names from a whole group of Heyer titles, with unmistakable Heyer phrases standing out among the romantic clichés. Once again, though the case was clear enough, their advisers counselled restraint, suggesting that their only recourse would be to leak the story to a columnist. This, of course, would have been totally out of character. Once again, they did nothing. But Georgette Heyer's publishers knew that she must never share advertising space with her plagiarist.

That was a winter of power cuts, and they decided to fly to Gibraltar for two weeks of convalescence from their colds. They planned to stay on, 'if life is too impossible in England. We are neither of us of an age, or in the right state of health, either to cope with life in a flat which has no light or heat other than is provided by electricity – let alone the lift! – or to be of the slightest use in a state of emergency. So the best we can do is to clear out. We are both looking forward with passionate longing to getting away from it all. Time was when I should have spurned with indignation any suggestion that I should clear out of England at such a moment, but there's nothing either of us can do, so we shall record our votes, and just GO!' They must both have voted for their old neighbour, Edward Heath, in that general election, and been desolated when he failed to form a government and gave way to Harold Wilson.

Georgette Heyer had another accident in Gibraltar and admitted to Reinhardt that the holiday had proved disappointing. It was their last one. In May, after a night of violent pain, she was admitted to Guy's Hospital, and cancer was diagnosed at last. It had already spread beyond her lungs, and there was nothing to be done but keep her as free from pain as possible for the twilight time that remained. She died on the fourth of July, leaving her husband totally lost. They had been married and he had been her constant support for almost fifty years.

Her bereaved fans learned her married name for the first time from her obituaries. The *Guardian* called her 'one of the great queens of historical fiction', the *Sunday Telegraph* said she was 'sometimes known as the 20th-century Jane Austen'; but *The Times* summed it up: 'She gave her name to a recognizable genre of fiction . . . Her family and many friends, together with her devoted readers, will be saddened to know that there can never be another Georgette Heyer to delight us.' In fact, a rumour soon sprang up that there were several unpublished novels among her papers, and her desolate husband did agree to the publication of *My Lord John* in 1975. After his death in 1976, her son allowed publication of *Simon the Coldheart* in 1977, very reasonably arguing that in this one case his mother, 'her own sternest critic', had been too harsh.

A measure of her popularity in the United States had been the proliferation of fake Heyers there, which, fortunately, did not reach its peak until after her death. For a while there was a real risk that they would destroy what they fed on, but it now seems unlikely. To turn from one of their cardboard copies to the elegant, ironic originals is to turn from candle to sunlight. In a few more years, the imitations will have sunk without trace, but Georgette Heyer's well-ordered world will still be there for those with the luck to find it. After her death, Rachel Law, Lady Ellenborough, sent an unsolicited tribute to her publishers. Georgette Heyer, she said, was the only reading for a hospital bed. 'Sex is cut down to size when the swish of the scythe sends a draught down the corridors . . . Comic characters are more enduring and archetypal than tragic ones. Tears may fall from heaven but laughter is the earth's underground, inexhaustible spring.' People like Lady Ellenborough, and the Romanian political prisoner, and many others, men and women, dons and lawyers and high-powered businessmen, will go on finding refreshment in Georgette Heyer's elegant romantic comedy and comfort in its strong moral framework. Highbrows who couple her books with the illiterate output of mass-market romancers merely betray that they have never read them. The romantic story is there, right enough, to keep children from play and old women from the chimney corner, but it is told with a style and humour that put her work in a class of its own. And the rules and customs of her private world can stand the test of time. She was not the only author of her day to create a private world as an escape from moral chaos. P. G. Wodehouse, C. S. Forester and Angela Thirkell did it too; Dick Francis still does, creating a small world at a time, as do the writers of science fiction. But romantic novelists write mainly for women, or are held to do so, and their form of escapism has never in this century achieved the status of the detective story, the sea tale, or science fiction.

If anyone could make the romantic novel respectable, it should have been Georgette Heyer, unacknowledged moralist and stylist extraordinary. It did not happen in her lifetime, and she minded silently, added her own denigration to that of the critics, indulged her mediaeval dream, and lived her intensely private life. In many ways, she was a very lucky woman. She made for herself the life she wanted; she combined career with marriage brilliantly; and she did not live to see the publication of *My Lord John*, and the end of her mediaeval dream. She wrote mainly for women, but lived all her life among men, whom she preferred. She gave an immense amount of pleasure to all kinds of people, and must have known she did. It would be a suitable irony, and no surprise, if a reappraisal in the next few years were to give her work the critical acclaim it never achieved in her lifetime. The need for escape is not likely to grow less.

Georgette Heyer's books

Dates given refer to first publication in Great Britain

Novels
Instead of the Thorn 1923, Hutchinson
Helen 1928, Longman
Pastel 1929, Longman
Barren Corn 1930, Longman

Historical romances
The Black Moth 1921, Constable, 1929, Heinemann
Powder and Patch (originally published as *The Transformation of Philip Jettan*) 1923, Mills & Boon, 1930, Heinemann
The Great Roxhythe 1923, Hutchinson, 1929, Heinemann
Simon the Coldheart 1925, Heinemann
These Old Shades 1926, Heinemann
The Masqueraders 1928, Heinemann
Beauvallet 1929, Heinemann
The Conqueror 1931, Heinemann
Devil's Cub 1932, Heinemann
The Convenient Marriage 1934, Heinemann
Regency Buck 1935, Heinemann
The Talisman Ring 1936, Heinemann
An Infamous Army 1937, Heinemann
Royal Escape 1938, Heinemann
The Spanish Bride 1940, Heinemann
The Corinthian 1940, Heinemann

Faro's Daughter 1941, Heinemann
Friday's Child 1944, Heinemann
The Reluctant Widow 1946, Heinemann
The Foundling 1948, Heinemann
Arabella 1949, Heinemann
The Grand Sophy 1950, Heinemann
The Quiet Gentleman 1951, Heinemann
Cotillion 1953, Heinemann
The Toll-Gate 1954, Heinemann,
Bath Tangle 1955, Heinemann
Sprig Muslin 1956, Heinemann
April Lady 1957, Heinemann
Sylvester: or the Wicked Uncle 1957, Heinemann
Venetia 1958, Heinemann
The Unknown Ajax 1959, Heinemann
A Civil Contract 1961, Heinemann
The Nonesuch 1962, Heinemann
False Colours 1963, Bodley Head
Frederica 1965, Bodley Head
Black Sheep 1966, Bodley Head
Cousin Kate 1968, Bodley Head
Charity Girl 1970, Bodley Head
Lady of Quality 1972, Bodley Head
My Lord John 1975, Bodley Head

Thrillers
Footsteps in the Dark 1932, Longman
Why Shoot a Butler? 1933, Longman
The Unfinished Clue 1934, Longman
Death in the Stocks 1935, Longman, 1953, Heinemann
Behold, Here's Poison 1936, Hodder & Stoughton, 1953,
    Heinemann
They Found Him Dead 1937, Hodder & Stoughton, 1953,
    Heinemann
A Blunt Instrument 1938, Hodder & Stoughton, 1954, Heinemann
No Wind of Blame 1939, Hodder & Stoughton

Envious Casca 1941, Hodder & Stoughton, 1955, Heinemann
Penhallow 1942, Heinemann
Duplicate Death 1951, Heinemann
Detection Unlimited 1953, Heinemann

Short stories
Pistols for Two 1960, Heinemann

Acknowledgements

Thanks are due to the following for permission to reproduce copyright illustrative material:

The Trustees of the British Museum for pp. xv, 21, 47 (left), 81, 85, 143.

The Victoria and Albert Museum for pp.25, 35, 52, 92.

The National Army Museum for p.47 (right).

The British Library for pp.109, 113.

The Trustees of the National Portrait Gallery for pp.63, 137.

The Mary Evans Picture Library for pp.18, 78, 99, 119, 164, 201.

Hamish Hamilton Ltd and Dennis Flanders for p.57.

The National Maritime Museum for p.116.

The Museum of London for p.140.

E. P. Dutton Inc for p.175.

Esquire Magazine for p.186.

Rod Delroy for p.190.

Thanks are due to Messrs William Heinemann Ltd for permission to quote freely from those books of Georgette Heyer published by them.

Many illustrations not specifically listed are from the Rougier family archives. The publishers have made every effort to trace all owners of copyright illustrative material. In the case of any omissions that have been unconsciously made the publishers apologize and invite those concerned to apply to the Random House Group for proper acknowledgement.

Index